SARAH MAE

THE COMPLICATED HEART

LOVING EVEN WHEN IT HURTS

B&H
PUBLISHING
NASHVILLE, TENNESSEE

Printed in the United States of America

978-1-4627-9698-4

Published by B&H Publishing Group
Nashville, Tennessee

Dewey Decimal Classification: 306.874

Subject Heading: MOTHER-DAUGHTER RELATIONSHIP /
PAIN / FORGIVENESS

Unless otherwise noted, all Scripture is taken from
the English Standard Version. ESV® Text Edition: 2016.
Copyright © 2001 by Crossway Bibles, a publishing
ministry of Good News Publishers.

Also used: New International Version (NIV), copyright
©1973, 1978, 1984, 2011 by Biblica, Inc.® Used by
permission. All rights reserved worldwide.

Cover illustration Adriana Badoi, *Thistle*, Courtesy Saatchi
Art. Author photo © Rebekah Viola Stoltzfus.

Published in association with D.C. Jacobson &
Associates, LLC, an Author Management Company,
www.dcjacobson.com.

1 2 3 4 5 6 7 • 23 22 21 20 19

Author's Note

These words reflect memories, and sometimes our memories are only true to us, but not perfectly true in reality.

I have tried to remember well, ask when I couldn't piece it all together, and sew up the pieces as best I could for the fullness of this testimony. Where I have gone wrong or where there is a tear or a string loose, I apologize. I have been as faithful as possible.

Some names have been changed for privacy reasons.

Contents

She Was Broken Too

Addendum

She broke me.
But He found me.
And after He bound up my wounds
He taught me how to love her.
Because *she was broken too.*

I waited patiently for the LORD;
he inclined to me and heard my cry.
He drew me up from the pit of
destruction,
out of the miry bog,
and set my feet upon a rock,
making my steps secure.
He put a new song in my mouth,
a song of praise to our God.
Many will see and fear,
and put their trust in the LORD.

(Ps. 40:1-3)

People Always Ask . . .

People always ask me how I forgave my mother.

How do you forgive someone who wounded you so deeply, who carelessly brushed aside your pain, who caused such destruction? And even more specifically, how do you forgive them when your wounds are still open, when they show no remorse, when you are so dang tangled up with them you're not sure how on earth to get untangled? How do you maintain a relationship with a toxic person? How do you not run for the hills, *sayonara*, peace out?

If you *should* run, how do you know *when* or *how*? How do you love your enemy when that enemy is your own mother or father or sibling or spouse? How do you get your emotional junk together so you can put a stop to the unhealthy patterns, behaviors, and habits you feel stuck in? Is it possible to get to the point where the pain no longer *consumes* you? And is there joy and victory in the midst of loss and unmet needs?

These are the questions I've sat next to, held, and walked with since I was fourteen years old—the year I moved in with my mom, the year I discovered that my mom was an alcoholic. This book is the answer to those questions, and even more specifically, it's what happened between the ages of fourteen and thirty-six.

You will experience my story *with me*, seeing through my eyes and hearing through my ears and perching on the ledge of my thoughts. You will also be able to peek behind the curtain into the heart of my mom through her journal entries and letters, which are at the end of many chapter. They give my mom a voice in this story.

The journal entries are not in order; I've just fit them in where I think it gives context to our intertwining lives. *It is a rare gift to be able to trace a life, to see what makes us fall and what makes us stand again.*

This is our story, the story of Mom and me, but it's also your story, and how even in great darkness light finds a way in, comforts us when we can't see, and leads us out into the fullness of day where redemption and freedom and healing are waiting for us. There is victory and hope and joy *despite the pain*.

Now, I know some of you reading this right now are in the dark. You think there is no way out, no way things could change, no way your tender heart could heal. Further, the very thought of forgiving and loving the person who hurt you the most sounds impossible. Some of you reading this right now are just *sad*—sad at what you missed out on, for what was taken from you, for the unfairness of it all. Your little-girl heart just wants to be loved by the person who was supposed to love you. It's a deep and often private ache, I know. Some of you have decided that to hope is just to hurt, and so you've placed hope in the attic, letting it collect dust, only holding onto it because you haven't wanted to bother with it. Hope is dangerous, and it's best kept tucked away.

It's for you I write this story.

For *all* of us, for all the torn-up and sad and ticked-off daughters, and the broken-hearted and the wounded ones just trying to figure a way through the mess.

I'm asking you to let hope sit in the same room with you while you read this book. You don't have to touch it yet. Just hang on to these truths for now: There are miracles and surprises and gifts even in the middle of the pain and the mess and complication of it all.

Dysfunction does not have to be your legacy. You may have been born into it, married into it, or created it yourself, but it does not have to be your destiny or your identity.

Victory is always on the table.

One Last, Very Important Thing

There is some graphic content in this book (not appropriate for children), and you may experience triggers—things that you read that may bring up painful memories or images. Because of this, here's what I'd like you to do before you slip into the story:

Evaluate. Assess your current emotional health and your age appropriateness, and decide if your heart is ready to embark on this type of material.

Pray. Pray for a willing and vulnerable heart; for protection over your heart, mind, and body; for eyes to see what God wants to reveal to you; and that His voice would be louder than the liar's voice.

Submit. Submit your heart to the Lord, or if you don't know Him, submit your heart to humbly receiving what He might have for you through this story.

Here we go.

Mom's Journal | Date unknown

I wish part of my purpose would be to write, to give something to others through my writing. God is just waiting for the right time for me to begin my new life . . .

She Broke Me

I Dare You

Sarah, age fourteen, Bowdon, GA, 1994

My fingers trace the shape of the cheap, pink Daisy razor sitting on the side of the tub. I wonder, *Can you slit your wrists with a cheap razor?*

Goose bumps form on my arms. My foot reaches up and turns the handle of the faucet, pushing it all the way to the red line, but only a cool stream comes out. I hear the scooping of ice cubes and the sound of them hitting her glass. The vodka comes next. My insides tighten and the feeling of steel moves up my shoulders and down my arms.

Her words from earlier loop in my brain. *I drink, so what, you need to get over it.*

So what.

Get over it.

I feel it again, the fire that's trapped under my skin, that burns through my body; I don't know how to get it out of me. I look at the razor again. Could I do it— could I slice the life out of myself? How much would it hurt? *How much would it hurt her?* My mind drifts off into a fantasy where Mom finds me limp and blue and slouched in red water. She realizes what she's done, how much she's destroyed, and she tries to wake me up but it's too late. Now *her* insides burn.

The fantasy dissipates, and I slide further into the water, which barely covers my shoulders.

What I want more than sliced arteries is for her to tell me she loves me. I want her to hold me in her arms as though I was her little girl again; I want her to rub my arms and stroke my hair and tell me everything is going to be okay. *The fire seethes.*

My fist wraps tightly around the razor and I yell out, "Maybe I'll kill myself!"

A split second of hope fills me, like maybe my insecure, needy declaration will wake her up and she'll run to me and we'll have that *real* talk and we'll cry and hug and prove talk show endings *really* do happen.

"Go ahead. *I dare you.*"

I release the razor and I sob into the lukewarm water.

She wins.

———

Sarah, age thirty-six, Port Richey, FL, 2016

God, please don't let her die alone.

She's quiet now. The off-and-on guttural yelling from last night in the hospital has stopped. They say dementia patients yell like that, but she doesn't have dementia; she's just dying, and this is her brain's response to it. She doesn't even know she's yelling; it's rhythmic. But now she's barely making a sound. Her eyes are open, but they just go back and forth, back and forth.

"Mom, please, if you can hear me, let me know."

Nothing. I hold her hand, rubbing my thumb over her rough, swollen skin. I put some music on, songs I know she loves, songs she had put on a CD for me years ago. "Sarah, you're the poet in my heart . . ."

"You give life, You give love, You bring light to the darkness. You give hope, You restore every heart that is broken. Great are You, Lord."

Over and over the same songs play quietly. Her eyes dart back and forth, and her breathing slows. Her eyes stop. I turn off the music and talk to her. I promise her I will tell our story, of what God has done. She always wanted to write, to help people, she said.

"You're almost there, Mom. Almost done. I'm right here with you. I love you."

My hand squeezes her hand and then I gently rub her head, her thin hair under my palms. And like a clock winding down, her breath just winds down. Slower and slower. I can feel her leaving.

And then, *her breath is gone.*

Just stillness.

On April 23, 2016 at 7:16 p.m. my mom took her last breath and entered the arms of Jesus.

CHAPTER 2

Home

It's the summer of '94 and I'm fourteen years old.

I'm skinny (the whole elbows and knees thing), a Judy Blume "Are You There God? It's Me, Margaret" bust exercise follower (it hasn't worked, *at all*), my hair is a mix between scraggly and puffy, and I have braces with dark blue bands on them because for some reason I thought that would look cool. *It doesn't.* I have small front teeth so now when I smile all you see is a line of dark blue. But I did start my period this summer, *finally*, so at least I can join the girls on the bus and talk about cramps. We feel so grown up.

Except I won't be on the bus when school starts, at least not here in Pennsylvania. I've convinced my dad to let me move to Georgia where my mom lives. *A teen girl should be with her mom, after all.* Mom told me I was old enough to decide who I wanted to live with, so even though I adored my dad, I boldly told him I wanted to go live with Mom. He didn't say much, but I saw the tears in his eyes. I knew it was hard for him, and I hate hurting him, but I need to be with my mom. I haven't lived with her since I was three, with the exception of a couple months every summer, per the custody agreement.

My parents divorced before I was a year old and my mom took me to live with her in Wasilla, Alaska. When I turned three my dad won custody of me and brought me back to Pennsylvania where I was born and where his parents lived. My mom said he got custody because he had more money, and my dad said my mom didn't really fight for me. He also told me he used to come home from work and I would be in my crib in a dirty diaper with three or four empty formula bottles around me, as though I hadn't been touched for hours. Mom said she used to just stare at the wall until she lost track of time. Sometimes she called a friend to come over and snort some cocaine, something to break up the monotony of staying home with me, of feeling all alone. She loved me, but she was also lonely.

My sister (who has a different dad) once told me that our Poppy, mom's dad, told her that I could have been born "retarded"[1] because Mom was probably using when she was pregnant with me. My teen sister bawled her sweet little eyes out as she told me this story. I pointed out to her that I was fine.

Of course, I have no recollection of cocaine or dirty diapers or staring at a wall next to my crib where I apparently spent hours with my bottles. I only have good memories of my mom, at least up to this point.

Spending summers with my mom was always a highlight for me; I have such wonderful recollections of those early years.

I remember the Little Rock Airforce Base where she lived with her fourth husband, Military Man, and where she worked at a youth center over the summer. I was twelve and I would ride my bike up there every day and buy pizza and Starbursts. In the mornings, all the kids at the center would stand and sing with the Whitney Houston version of the National Anthem. Mom drove the bus for the center to and from the pool for the kids, and it was always a wild ride. (She was known for taking curves a little too fast.) The kids loved my mom and called her, "Ms. Susan." I was so proud that she was my mom.

I remember being a little girl, five years old, lying in bed with her before I could read, holding a book and copying her. I'd watch her curl her fingers around a chunk of her hair while reading, and I'd mimic her until it became my own lifelong habit (reading *and* playing with my hair).

I remember all the years before I was thirteen staying up late into those summer nights rearranging furniture until I fell asleep on a chair at 2:00 a.m., and her reading library books to me and us watching Hulk Hogan together and going to movies and laughing hysterically with each other. I remember days at the pool where she would play in the water with me, and there were water park visits and Toys R Us trips and talking late at night as she tenderly scratched my arms as I fell asleep.

I wanted to be just like my mom when I grew up. Well, *her or Madonna*, but mostly her. She was the best and I thought I was the luckiest.

Hello Georgia

Before I board the plane and head to my new life in Georgia, I hug my dad.

He has tears in his eyes and doesn't say much, he just squeezes me harder and then lets me go.

Mom picks me up from the airport and we drive the hour from Atlanta to the small town of Bowdon, Georgia (population 2,001). We turn onto Mill Street and less than a minute later I see it, the simple beige one-story house with maroon shutters and a front porch swing. Mom parks the light-blue Ford Windstar in the driveway, stopping just in front of the detached two-car garage.

I follow Mom up the back steps and into the cluttered, carpeted screened-in porch. Up against the back wall, by the door to the house, there are two old, worn armchairs, both which would be an eyesore anywhere else, but somehow fit perfectly in this well-loved space. Between the chairs is a glass table with random papers scattered on it, partially covering a gray film. Ashes from a few poorly aimed flicks of a cigarette lie next to a butt-filled ashtray.

Next to the door and catty-corner to the chairs is a ragged light-blue and faded pink love seat with a ripped seat, exposing a slice of the yellow foam beneath it. A man with a kind, crooked-tooth smile,

mile-long eyelashes, and a brown curly mullet stands on the porch in front of us. "This is John!" Mom says, enthusiastically introducing me to her twenty-one-year-old live-in boyfriend, twenty years my mom's junior. He takes my bags and asks me if I'd like something to eat—a sandwich maybe? *Yes, please.*

Mom and I sit down, her in the armchair closest to the front door and me on the couch. She pulls out a cigarette, places it between her lips, and looks cross-eyed as she lights it. She sucks in, breathes out, and leans forward with a huge smile on her face. *I love her so much.* We talk and laugh like old friends; we're just so giddy to be together. The screen door to the house opens and Buddy, my mom's part-Bluetick hound, gleefully runs onto the porch, John following behind balancing a grilled sandwich loaded with ham and lettuce and mayo and drinks for him and Mom. Mom scrunches Buddy's face in her hands and baby-talks to him while I dig into my sandwich.

Sitting here on this smoky screened-in porch, surrounded by random objects like the ceramic angels that sit on the wood ledges, I am struck by the joy of it all. I relax into the ragged couch and smile; *I'm home.*

Mom's Journal | 1993 | One year before I moved in with her

My purpose is clear. I know what must be accomplished in order to survive. I've come to the place ... here, I must open all wounds, bear the string of memories, recall what had to happen to bring me down and make me cry. It is time to discard what I believe I learned with each encounter. I must reach for the true lessons ... those I've denied all my life for the sake of retaining my dignity and pride. It is time to admit I have no pride, and there is no dignity in the life of a foolish woman. In order to sidestep the inevitable fall I face, I will look at, and face the ugliness I have been running from—I will lean on the good, and cast aside the bad whenever it tries to interfere with the good feelings—most of all, I will pray to God for His help and strong hands.

Feeling the pain you own is okay.

It can't be overridden with anger or denials, or vengeance. It will always be inside you, no matter how much you convince yourself it's not affecting how you feel. Best bet: embrace the pain, own it, for it is real. Flowing with what's inside your heart loses the ache; comforts the disappointment. It is there. Why deny it of its expression?

CHAPTER 3

Always Drunk

His hand is on my neck, just below my chin. His fingers and thumb tighten with increasing intensity, and I can't swallow.

Mom is driving, John is in the passenger seat, and I'm in the middle of the back, leaning forward, my head between the front seats. I have pushed him too far. I knew I was crossing a line, making one too many smart-aleck comments, but the quickness in which his hand grabs my neck startles me. John has never laid a hand on me before, or my mom that I know of.

I stare at him with haughty, daring eyes. *He has the fire too.* Ten seconds go by, his grip tightens with one last show of dominance, and he lets go. Mom doesn't say a word.

I'm careful not to push John again.

It's only been a few months since I've moved in.

Mom and John adore each other and have created a world that they alone inhabit. My sister and I aren't a part of this world; we're just tethered to it, but we float out on our own, alone. They are always drunk.

Mom starts her morning with a tall glass of vodka (or whiskey) and 7Up. I don't know what John drinks, but sometimes he sneaks into the kitchen when my mom's gone, and drinks liquor straight from the bottle. Once they start drinking, they keep going all day unless Mom has to go to work. She tries to cover the smell of alcohol by chewing gum and misting herself with body spray. She can function while drunk. She doesn't sway or slur her words. But the more she drinks, the meaner she gets.

When I came home from school today, I smiled at her and she told me I was so ugly with my braces. I close my mouth.

Home is no longer grilled sandwiches and huge *so happy to be with you* smiles. The giddiness has worn away and the joy that filled up my whole being in the first few weeks of being here has been replaced by despair and confusion.

Loving affection is rare.

Touch is her body pushing mine into my bedroom after a fight, me grabbing her shirt as I fall to the floor, and her punching my head until I let go.

She has only laid a strong hand on me a couple of times. Her weapon is not her hands but her *words*. She knows my weakness and she attacks it. She sees

I'm sensitive, so she makes a point to make fun of me in every fight we have. She knows just how to cut me.

"You're so stupid."

"You're so ugly."

"You're such a [expletive]."

"Look at your ankles! What's wrong with them?"

She laughs at me.

Her verbal genius consists of masterful sarcasm and an ability to convince you that you are the dumbest, most incompetent person she's ever been around. After she cuts you down over and over again, you get angry and the fire inside you rises. Once this happens, she gets self-righteously calm—so, *so calm*—and as you reel from her smugly spoken passive-aggressive comments, she slides into the role of victim. *Why are you yelling? Why are you so angry? You have a problem.* You are now in an alternate reality where you can no longer tell what is up and what is down. You see the blood from the cuts, but you're still convinced maybe it's your fault, maybe there really isn't even a cut and you're just crazy.

You blame yourself, believing that you *really* are dumb. You hate yourself for being this way and you begin to verbally berate yourself. You add to the cuts.

This is the rhythm of home, and it always ends with punching or scratching yourself and screaming with a clenched jaw so no one hears the cry.

———

I go in and out of Mom and John's orbit, depending on when they decide to invite me into it.

Tonight, not only am I invited in, but I'm offered a new role to play. Instead of the confused, sad, hopeless, angry teenager role, I will join the two-, now three-party, cast and play the role of mother.

Before the invite, I'm in Ranburne, Alabama (only ten minutes from home) at the roller-skating rink. My sister Keitha and I come here on Friday nights whenever we can get a ride.

It's dark here and the lights are flashing neon colors over the skating rink. Billy Ray Cyrus's "Achy Breaky Heart" is blaring through the speakers and I make a move and go from skating forwards to backwards, then immediately scan the rink to see if anyone saw me handle these skates like a boss. I'm singing the chorus loud, my hair is blowing beside my face, and I'm pretty sure I'm being checked out. I skate over to the edge of the rink with a slight grin on my face. I skate-walk over to the food area and sit in one of the booths. It's here that someone tells me I'm getting a ride home, and to be outside waiting. I don't know why I have to leave early, but I take my skates off and wait in the parking lot. My ride pulls up and I get in.

I am told that John has torn up our house.

As soon as I get home I walk up the front porch steps and through the glow of the flashing red and blue lights. Mom is right inside the front door talking with a police officer.

"Do you want to press charges?"

"No."

I think maybe I'm in a dream. I float through Mom and John's chaotic world where chairs with newly broken legs are turned over and pictures are smashed and curtains are lying on the floor next to the broken glass from the coffee table. The officer leaves. Mom sits down on the one piece of furniture in the living room John didn't flip over, the couch. I float back to the body by the door—my body—and sink back into it, realizing this is not a dream. This is our life.

Mom is small now. There is no sarcasm or verbal jabs, no passive-aggressive comments. She's alone even with me beside her. She's shaking, so I put my arms around her. I rub her head, smooth her hair, and tell her it's all going to be okay. Her eyes don't move from the wall. She's scared. I am her comfort. She is the child now and I am the mother.

This is the whiplash cycle of our relationship. I am either mothering her after a fight with John or with her condescending father, or I am the target of her verbal assaults, left alone to lick my own wounds.

No one is mothering me.

————

My *ex-stepbrother* Shawn moves in with us.

I want to impress him because he's older than me and I think he's cute and I want him to think I'm cool. My mom thinks he's wonderful; she's always wanted a son. The last time I saw him was when I was twelve and he was sixteen. I was visiting my mom in

Arkansas, when she lived on the Little Rock Base with her fourth husband, Military Man; Shawn is his son.

One night, while I was lying down on the couch and my mom and Military Man were, *I don't know where*, Shawn sat down with me. He talked to me gently and then slowly began rubbing my legs, inching higher and higher up my thighs awakening something in me, something that shouldn't have been awakened at twelve years old.

Now I'm fourteen and he's eighteen, and for some reason my mom puts him in my room, maybe because I have bunk beds. We stay up late every night talking about his former gang life in Guam (where his mother is from) and his time in LA where he was a member of the Crips, which stands for cripple. He tells me that their rival gang the Bloods, were known for killing, while the Crips were known for crippling people. He teaches me to write in the style of the Crips. I'm fascinated with his stories.

One night he pulls his pants down and tells me he thinks he looks good. I've never seen this before and I'm shy. Our nightly talks have moved to my top bunk, where it's no longer just me anymore. I remember back to being twelve as I lie down and he puts his hands on my legs. He knows what he's doing. He's good at it.

I think this is normal. He likes me. I feel special. I have no idea that he is taking advantage of me, that it's wrong for an eighteen-year-old man to put his hands on a fourteen-year-old girl. I have no idea how his hands will make his way into my marriage and how I will struggle for years to feel safe enough to be touched without separating from my body. I don't know any of this because I'm naïve and young and I just want to be loved.

One night I'm waiting up for him because he hasn't come home yet. Mom is at work at an overnight job, and I don't want to be alone. The porch floor creaks. He's home. Shawn wobbles in and sways as he moves toward me, drunk. I smile. He falls on me and now I'm on my bedroom floor and his hands are working at the button on my jeans. I perch onto my elbows and his hot breath is in my face, rank with alcohol. "Shawn, stop." I don't feel scared; *he won't do anything. Will he?* I'm inching backwards and his hands are trying to pull down my unbuttoned pants. His head moves down my belly. He stops. I feel air over me as his body is no longer holding me down. He runs to the bathroom across the way from my room and I hear the sounds of whatever he drank that night pour out of him. I get up, button my pants, and crawl into bed. He's back in my room now, but he falls into the bottom bunk bed and passes out.

After a few weeks he moves out, and I beg him to stay. *The heart is odd.* He promises me he'll come back. I never see him again.

Letter from Mom to her dad | July 31, 1971 | seventeen years old

Dear Father,

I know that you and Mother both have tried to bring me up to a well-adjusted, average teen-age girl, and in my eyes that is really what I am. But you definitely do not think so, as you per-haps would leave some decisions up to me, and I speak of decisions—not about whether I should obey you or decide things for myself. But those are matters which, I believe, have time and again come up in our few serious discussions with no comprehension from either of us. I blame every-thing entirely on me, since I have not tried hard enough to abide by your rules. I am sure you have much to say along these lines.

But you both know, no matter how much we talk of such things, nothing is ever settled, thus is the reason for my letter, for I believe it will "do away" with much needless arguments and accusations. I have caused you both much pain and anxiety, I know—but I want you both to understand that I have not meant to, and besides whatever you may think of me now, I am a good girl.

Father, you told me I had two choices—going with you or packing my things and simply leaving. Well, that I must do—you see, in your eyes I have done so much wrong that you are sure I must go with you on the trip. I swear to God alone I believe I have not warranted such a decision from you. I get "in trouble" with you mostly because of the hours I keep lately, yet as you notice I have a job, am taking a course which I believe can be useful to me, and that I have, at least, attempted to please you in these ways by doing a good job, and making high grades.

This letter to you, Father, is an attempt at an explanation of my feelings that I know will be difficult for you to understand. You see, I realize you have been great parents, but you know that no matter how much you have tried to teach me, I always end up learning the hard way through experiences. I know there are many thoughts running through your head as to the possible stupidity of this letter, but I felt I should write it to let you know how much I really love you, and because of that love, I think I must be punished, or disciplined, but by the hardest way I know: to get out and find out for myself. It is the most I can do for you, and I know it will be a great burden from your shoulders. I don't want it to be this way, but since I believe in what I have been saying, I believe this is the best for you and Mother. Always remember I love you. Please try and believe that I am good . . .

Susan

CHAPTER 4

The Intervention

She's on the screened-in porch, cigarette between her fingers, drink in hand.

Buddy is lounging on the porch at her feet. My hands push open the screen door and I step down into the porch and sit on the old couch catty-corner to my mom.

"I have to talk to you about something."

She inhales deep and flicks the ashes. Her dirty blonde hair is parted down the middle and thin wisps scraggle down past her shoulders. She's a thick woman, pretty, with an inch-long indent on her forehead from when her dad kicked her into the edge of a table. Her skin is tan and dotted, and she has a slight gap between her two front teeth. I miss hugging her. The last time I tried to hug her she pushed me away asking if I was a lesbian.

I'm about to have an intervention with her about her drinking.

I saw a show on TV where the host helped stage an intervention for a family who had an alcoholic family member. The family member was upset but agreed to get help. Everyone was crying and hugging. This is what I'll do: I'll confront Mom about her drinking and she will see how it affects her and how much she hurts me and she will decide to get help. This is the answer. Once she knows the truth, her eyes will be open.

"What is it, Sarah?"

Heat is crawling up my neck and into my head. I smile because I'm nervous. "I think . . . maybe . . . I've noticed that . . . I think . . . Mom, you're an *alcoholic.*"

She laughs. She doesn't understand?

"Mom, when you drink, and you drink a lot, you get really mean. And I think you're an alcoholic."

"So what?"

So what?

"Mom, you don't care that you are an alcoholic and that you are so mean when you drink? You really hurt me."

Eye roll.

"Oh, Sarah, I drink, so what—you need to get over it."

Another drink, another drag; *she's not interested.*

She's not taking me seriously. What can I say that will make her care?

"Honestly, Mom, you're just so mean and . . . I don't think I love you anymore."

She laughs again. My insides start to burn; her nonchalance . . . the oxygen.

————

I step into the bathtub. I entertain thoughts of opening my veins and letting the fire out with the blood. I yell out to Mom that maybe I'll just kill myself. End it all here, alone. *Will she care then?*

She yells back, "Go ahead. I dare you."

A Light in the Dark

One day my uncle Mark, one of my mom's brothers, visits us. He's a large man with a large brown mustache and a low, loud voice. He peeks his head into my room and tells me he has something I might like. He hands me a cassette tape of some singer named Clay Crosse. "Thanks," I say. I toss it aside when he walks out. I turn up my Boyz II Men album and go back to my own world.

Later that night I see the cassette tape on my floor and decide to check it out. I put it on as background music while I clean my room. Once my room is straightened up, I head up to my top bunk to write. It's here, in this bed and in these pages, that I offer my heart. When I write, the fire in me calms. I set my pen down and attune my senses to the music. I listen to the words.

> *So many years, so confused. Wondering*
> *where I'm going to . . .*
> *And I have been missing something in my*
> *life . . .*[2]

This, these words, they are calling up to the surface something deep in my soul. *God is here.*

I believe in God. When my sister was taken by her dad a few years ago and they disappeared, and Mom didn't know where they were, I prayed every night from my bed in Pennsylvania that she would be found. "God, please, please help Mom find Keitha." I know people go missing every day and terrible things happen, wicked things, and we don't know why it seems God answers some prayers and doesn't answer others. I don't understand the full gravity of good and evil and the battle that surrounds us, and how sometimes it seems that evil wins, even though in the end evil will never win.

What I know is that nearly a year after my sister went missing, Mom found her. And my belief in a God who hears my prayers was cemented in my heart. Yes, I believe in God, but I don't think I *know* Him. But my soul does; my soul knows something of Him that my mind and my heart has not yet understood. All I know is that right now I'm crying and asking God for whatever it is that the man on the tape is singing about. I want that kind of *something*, to find myself in something.

> Deep calls to deep
> at the roar of your waterfalls;
> all your breakers and your waves
> have gone over me.
> (Ps. 42:7)

My Heart Is Primed

Mom has a Bible laid open on her bed. She's sitting up, her legs under the covers, her glasses on. Her beer is on the table next to her bed. She smiles at me and I snap a picture of her.

Mom tells me that she was in a car accident years ago, that her Jeep flipped, and the top was crushed into the seats. She shows me the picture of the smashed Jeep. A man she had met was with her—she was giving him a ride when the accident happened. They both walked away unharmed. The man slept on the couch at her parents' house the night of the accident, and the next day he was gone. She was convinced he was an angel.

––––––

Mark says he wants to take us to church. I've only ever been to a Catholic church, the one I went to every Sunday with my stepmom. I did not like going because it was boring, and sitting still was extremely difficult for me. I was constantly fidgeting, playing with my hair, looking around. My stepmom would tell me to stop it. "Be still." I spent more time focusing on keeping my hands down and my body forward than paying attention to the priest.

All to say, I'm not super enthused about going to church.

We pull up in the church parking lot and the first thing I notice is that the building doesn't look like the Catholic church building I'm used to. Where are the stained glass windows? We walk up the steps and the doors are opened for us by an African American man with a giant smile on his face. "Welcome!"

I smile back, but before I can say, "Thank you," my senses are overwhelmed with what I see and hear, and the words never make it out of my lips. I walk forward into a colorful sea of people clapping and singing, smiling, *in church*, and I'm dumbstruck. What is this?

I've never seen anything like it, just like I had never heard music about God that wasn't a hymn. I thought all churches were Catholic, but apparently, I'm wrong. All that keeps going through my mind as I continue walking down the aisle is, even though I don't really understand it, *the Spirit is here*. I join the clapping and the smiling, and when we sit, I have no problem listening.

The man who is speaking captures my full attention, and he speaks in a way that I can comprehend. God knows I need these people and their smiles and their exuberance.

Some people experience God in the calm, ancient liturgical tradition. But for me, for now, this is how God speaks to me. And *I'm captivated*.

Before my uncle Mark leaves, he gives me a book of Bible verses for different topics. I can look up loneliness, for example, and there are several verses listed about that topic.

I sit in the bathtub for hours and read that little orange book.

Light has stepped into the pit, quietly sitting down next to me.

Mom's Journal | 1986 | I'm six and my dad has custody of me and Mom has custody of my sister

As if I didn't know it already, it's tough handling your child all alone. I do most all of it here with Dad, but sometimes I sure wish he'd help out. I think that's why God figured two people make babies, perhaps so both would share in the upbringing. I've handled it twice on my own . . . I do okay except the times I lose my temper and yell. These are the roughest times for me. Another problem—I wish I had someone to talk to . . . I'm feeling pretty much alone and, of course, lonely. Not that that is anything new . . . I don't like myself very much anymore, and I need someone to tell me why I should.

There's a lot of pain to deal with here or there, for that matter. I figure this is in God's plan for me now, and I think it's going to get worse before it gets better. But if it's God's plan (and it is), I will deal with it the best I can, so there!

I wish I would have been a good wife so my children wouldn't have to be without a mom-and-dad family. Again, I'm a loser. I must be the best I can as a single provider and earn their respect from my job as a mother exclusively. SO BE IT. God, be with me and help me to find my way.

CHAPTER 5

Culture Shock

Kids here are different than kids in Pennsylvania.

I'm in eighth grade and I show up to school in a plaid shirt, light baggy jeans, navy-blue Converse sneakers, and a backpack slung over one shoulder. My hair is down, still wet from my shower, and I don't have any makeup on. It becomes obvious that I missed a memo on how girls are supposed to dress here. The girls wear curled ponytails tied up in a bowed ribbon. Their shirts are tucked into their nicely rolled-up jean shorts with purses bouncing off their hips. Lips are colored rose and eyelashes are coated long and black. I'm immediately out of place, but the fact that I'm new *and* from the North gets me attention. Before class begins, Hannah Haines, one of the popular girls, pulls up a chair across from my desk to meet me.

"Hi, I'm Hannah!"

Her blonde bangs sit right above her dark-blue eyes. Her ponytail is one perfect curl.

"Hi," I say back.

"What's your daddy do?"

I'm still getting used to the Southern drawl, and I haven't called my dad "daddy" since I was about three years old. *I have so much to learn here.* Hannah is kind to me. I find out that her *daddy* is a local doctor. She's best friends with a girl named Shelby who wears her curls down. Hannah just broke up with Ray, a black boy. The rumor was that her daddy found out about them and that's why they broke up. In this town, for some reason, black boys going out with white girls will get you a side-eye and head shake. *Shame, shame, shame.*

In gym class a boy comes up to me and calls me a Yankee. I've never been called that before and don't really understand it. At lunch, the conversation centers on the Civil War and why the South should have won. This is all so weird to me.

The black kids mostly hang out with black kids and the white kids hang out with white kids. There are so many rebel flags.

"You ain't a [expletive]-lover are you?" I stare dumbfounded at the boy who asks me this, wondering if he really just used the "n" word.

I feel like I'm in another world.

———

I don't fit here, and it doesn't help that I'm socially awkward. I don't know this culture, I don't speak their language, I don't wear a purse or ribbons, I don't understand the rebel flags or being called names for being friends with black people, and I'm dreadfully insecure. I avoid Hannah and Shelby and the rebel boys. At lunch I sit with Claire, a tall, pale girl who has long blonde hair that reaches to her lower back. She shakes her head in quick movements when she talks, kind of like a bobble head. I don't think she has many friends. We also sit with Tasha, a black girl. Tasha has short hair and wears dirty sweatpants with a stained plain T-shirt that tends to ride up and show pieces of her heavy-set body. Tasha and I have gym class together and it's here that we get to know each other and become friends. Neither of us like gym class and we often find an excuse to sit on the bleachers and talk. We mostly talk about boys.

At home, my mom warns me about how people view black people here. She tells me to be careful or I'll be labeled a [expletive]-lover.

I meet Jason in school.

He's an outsider too. He's a white boy who dresses in baggy jeans, a tucked-in polo shirt, and a brown braided belt that hangs halfway down his thigh. His pale face is dotted with freckles and he has stiff brown hair slicked into a smooth bump at the top of his forehead. The rest of his head is shaved. He's shorter than me. We start to hang out. He comes over to my house or I go over to his apartment, or we just walk around town together, just the two of us.

Mom doesn't seem to care where I go or what I do, so long as I'm home for the night. When I come home, she's usually sipping her vodka and watching *Current Affairs* or some similar show. She stays in front of the TV for hours, only getting up to make another drink or let Buddy out.

She likes to cook during the commercials, so I always come home for dinner.

Jason lives in the Wood Ridge apartments, a low-income housing community. He lives in the apartment right next to the one mom used to live in several years earlier. It's in this apartment that Mom used to dress Keitha and I alike. Then she'd drop us off at another apartment and go to work. On one occasion the two sisters who took care of me and my sister had fresh lash marks all over their legs. They told us their daddy beats them with a belt or a stick when they do something wrong. They ask us, "What does your daddy hit you with?"

"My dad has never hit me," I tell them. They're baffled. Keitha doesn't say a word.

It was also here, in 1989, that my four-year-old little sister was taken away from my mom because of a devastating accusation, one I'll ask my mom about a few years from now, one that keeps me from visiting Mom that summer. It isn't until years later that I learn the story of what happened that year, and the years surrounding it. By the time I learn, the shrapnel has already shattered so much of our lives.

Jason lives here with his crack-addicted mom and her crack-addicted boyfriend.

His dad left him and his older sister and brother when they were little, and they haven't seen him since. I don't know much about poverty or crack, but I know it's the first time I've seen someone have to wear his girlfriend's sneakers because his mom can't afford to buy him shoes. Good thing we're the same shoe size.

What Jason and I don't get at home we get from each other. We become each other's refuge. We are inseparable. He sneaks over to my house every night to sleep with me. He crawls in through my window onto the top bunk. One night Mom comes into my room and I swear she sees his body hiding close to me under the covers. I smile nervously because I think I'm caught, but I'm not that worried about her reaction. I mean, I pretty much do whatever I want. I'll never know what she would have done because she never catches him.

We have sex. I never question the morality of this because I don't know there's anything to question or consider. All I know is that this is what couples do, and we're a couple, so it's what we do. Even though I'm only fourteen, I feel grown up. Mom never says she knows, but she makes a comment about making sure to use protection.

———

Mom has always been open with me about sex.

One morning, before I meet Jason, before Shawn ever comes to stay with us, I saunter into mom's bedroom and plop onto her bed with my elbows propped up and my head in my hands. She's hanging up her clothes.

I want to know what she was like as a teenager, so I ask her. She tells me she was a hippie child, a flower girl, and that for Halloween one year she wore a long, sleeveless dress with the words, "The Acid Queen" painted on the front. She told me she was in love with a boy named Billy Hooker, but her dad made her break up with him after Billy took her out on his motorcycle and they got hit in a hit-and-run accident. Doctors told Mom she would never walk again because of the damage done to her foot, including the loss of her pinky toe. After months of therapy, and likely some grit, she learned to walk again—although every now and then her foot will get "stuck" while she's walking, and she has to stop or limp the rest of the way.

I bring up a picture that I saw of her as a teenager, one of her in a bikini, and I notice her figure.

"Mom, how did you deal with having a small chest when you had a boyfriend? Weren't you worried about it?" *I was worried about it.*

"No, Sarah, guys don't care about that."

She picks up a cigarette from her dresser and lights it up. Smoke wraps around her as she looks at me.

"Guys only care about one thing, and it's not your chest size."

With that, she turns back to her clothes and, with her cigarette hanging from her lips, continues hanging them up.

Mom's Journal | November 5, 1986 | Mom is stressed and lonely and might lose custody of my sister as well

I must admit late last night I finally burst in tears and from deep within my heart I acknowledged just how VERY MUCH I DO HURT from this divorce. I mean, when I kicked K out, I only concentrated on the relief of no longer "walking the borders" of control. It wasn't until last night I admitted to myself the extremity of my emotional commitment to the relationship—how much I'd counted on everything turning out alright—how extreme was my denial that it wouldn't somehow work out. I was amazed that up to that point I'd been un-feeling and unreceptive to such disappointment—topped with almost unbearable anger for the totally uncalled for, RUDE, DEGRADING remarks I actually held a phone to my ear and listened to . . . that little girl, the one who put herself through such pain and rejection and utter loneliness all because she'd never felt a sense of being worthy of love simply for herself—her special self. Was there no one she had to turn to, to count on where one could feel, I mean really feel, she'd be loved simply because she was she—without any other conditions for love that would warrant the attentions and regard the basic care that she's feeling actually mattered in her? My therapist says, "Cry for that little girl, Susan, cry for her loneliness and lack of somewhere to turn when her heart was breaking as she must have suffered too much, then burying that pain without ever acting as if it were real and valid, but instead, acting as if it was only another reason she must not deserve happiness, only guilt and all the blame. HOW VERY SAD. POOR, POOR DEAR SUSIE."

CHAPTER 6

Get This Town Off of Me

I've been here for almost two years now.

John moved out a while ago, sometime between him going into a rage (after pouring her alcohol down the sink just to get a rise out of Mom) and him getting so drunk in public the cops had to take him to jail for a night. Mom hates drunks who can't handle their liquor.

Mom started dating Marty, a man her age who has two daughters a few years younger than me. Marty has his own place, a double-wide trailer, so they take turns getting drunk between the two.

Jason and I are still together.

Mom and I mostly stay away from each other, but tonight while doing the dishes, I'm so distracted by my anger toward her because of some cutting remark she made, that I accidently slice my thumb open with a knife. It won't stop bleeding. There is a flap of skin and what looks like bone underneath. I wrap some paper towels around it and go to the screened-in porch where Mom is sitting. By the time I open the door, the paper towels are already red.

"I think I need to go to the hospital. I cut my thumb open." Mom just looks at me.

"We're not going to the hospital."

"Mom! It won't stop bleeding!

She's looking out toward the backyard. She doesn't say anything else. She sure as heck doesn't get up and try to help me. *Whatever.*

I go back in and wrap some Band-Aids around it, but they don't stop the blood. I finally get some tape and wrap it around a wad of paper towels. When I wake up in the morning and slowly pull the paper towels back, it starts to bleed again.

There's a scar and a painful sensitivity in that thumb even today that reminds me that even healed wounds, when hit just right, still hurt.

Sixteen and Pregnant

It's spring of '96 and I, yes I, the non-ribbon girl, try out and (barely) make the cheerleading squad. I'm not very good though, so I'm only able to cheer for the middle school team even though I'm a ninth grader. A couple of my friends make fun of me when

I wear a ribbon in my ponytail the day after I make the team; they think it's funny that I'm a cheerleader now. It is so unlike me, and truth be told, I don't know why I tried out for the team. I do like the outfits, the crisp feel of the uniform and the sharp red and white colors. I guess I just wanted a change; I guess I just want to belong.

There's just one problem that abruptly announces itself while I'm eating Froot Loops in my bedroom before school. I don't yet know this problem, but I know I'm throwing up my breakfast.

And . . . my period is late. *Oh crap.*

Jason and I drive to the store in the car my dad drove down to me on my sixteenth birthday (an '89 Plymouth Sundance Duster with three-spoke chrome wheels). He gets me a pregnancy test, I take it, and we drive to the church parking lot up the road from my house to see the results.

Pregnant.

I throw the test out the window. Jason jumps out of the car and goes and gets it. *This can't be happening.* Heat is filling up my chest and my ears. I look at my hands; they speak for me as they wobble. Unsteady. Pressure filling my head. *I have to go home.*

———

The health clinic is huge and there are so many people. I drive here the day after throwing the pregnancy test out the window. After I see the doctor and he confirms my pregnancy, I am led to the lady with the WIC forms. *Yes, we'll be needing assistance.* I'm going to have a baby at sixteen.

After getting home from the clinic the phone rings and my mom and I pick up at the same time. The woman's voice on the other end says, "This is *so and so* calling from the health clinic, is this a good time?" I say no and hang up, but it's too late, my mom heard the woman. She called me to her room, where I sat on her bed and told her I was pregnant. She froze. And then, she checked out, as though I didn't even tell her.

That night I called my grandmother Julie, my dad's mom, who I was close to, and who sent me money every month "just for fun." I told her I was pregnant, and she said she'd have it taken care of. The sound of the dial tone told me she wasn't pleased when I told her I was keeping the baby.

Next, I called my dad, and he was gentle and kind and said, "Maybe it will be fun to have a little one running around." It was all going to be okay.

Jason and I will get married and get a little apartment and start a family. It will be hard, but doable.

We are having a baby.

———

It's a good thing the plane to Pennsylvania was near empty and no one was sitting next to me because I pretty much hurled the whole flight. This pregnancy sickness is intense.

After my dad and I get home, my dad tells me he hasn't told my stepmom yet and that I should tell her. Great.

I sit on the carpeted steps in front of the bathroom where she's doing her nightly routine. I tell her. I say the words I have to keep saying.

I'm pregnant.

I'm pregnant.

I'm pregnant.

She hugs me. It's awkward because we don't have a close relationship.

All of this is awkward though because I'm sixteen and pregnant.

The next day I see my grandmother at work, the family dealership, but she won't look at me. My dad tells me later that after I told her I was pregnant she said to him, "Our little girl is in trouble." Dad says she'd jump off a cliff for me. But today, she won't even look at me. It's like I'm dead to her. *What a way to start the summer.*

———

Three months pregnant and daily puking and *I'm so over this*. Will it ever end? My stepmom wants the baby to raise as her own, as my brother or sister. This is so weird to me and I can't even imagine it. I'm willing to give the baby up for adoption, but not to her. Then there's this whole other bizarre scenario my family suggests where I'm sent to New Jersey to live with an aunt until I have the baby. I feel like I'm in another universe. I'm just here like, "Does anyone care what I think?"

It's exhausting fighting for something no one believes in or supports you in. Jason is in Georgia and my one and only friend who knew about the baby has no idea how to talk to me about it. We're young and just think it's cool that my chest is getting bigger. The weight of the situation feels a million miles away.

But you know what doesn't feel like a million miles away? The feeling of being alone, unloved, sick, and invisible. So the minute my mom's mom (Grandma) drives to Pennsylvania from Georgia to see me, shows me love by sitting next to me on my bed and putting her arm around me (oh sweet comfort) and telling me *I really should have an abortion*, I say yes, in utter relief that now I will be wanted.

She goes back to Georgia and I call my grandmother Julie to "have it taken care of."

And so, in the summer of 1996, after holding my three-month newly swelled belly and saying to the baby through sobs, "I'm so sorry, please forgive me," I have an abortion.

My dad takes me to the hospital where the doctor suggests I have the abortion and where he can put me under completely, so I don't feel a thing.

At the hospital I don't check in under my name, but under the name Sandy Charles. Sarah Clark (my maiden name) isn't having an abortion today, Sandy is. *No one will know the family secret.*

My dad holds my hand and never leaves my side except for the actual procedure. Afterward he takes me to my grandmother Julie's house to stay.

I sleep for two days and wake up in my grandmother Julie's house, the one who wouldn't talk to me before but who is now smiling at me from across the table where I sit for breakfast. We never speak about the abortion. I only know I'm living with my grandmother Julie because my stepmom now hates me for what I have done. We always had a tense relationship, but now it's in the gutter.

———

I move back to Georgia, back to Jason, back to my alcoholic mom, back to the *same old*.

I come home from school one day and Mom tells me she and Marty are married. *Surprise!* They last a month before they get a divorce. This is my mom's fifth divorce.

Jason is still in the picture, but I don't love him. He's just my boyfriend because he *just is*. His home life has gotten worse so I rent a trailer for him for only $150 a month. I pay for it with the money my grandmother Julie sends me each month. I paint the cabinets and buy cheap furniture and bring in groceries. I still live with my mom, technically, but spend a ton of time at the trailer playing house. Eventually I realize I don't want to spend all my time with Jason, so I start staying home, doing laundry, cleaning my room, and cozying up for a good show. By myself. I like it. Jason hates it.

I head over to the trailer one afternoon while Jason is at work and there are two cars parked outside. I walk in, open the first guest bedroom door, and see a naked man and woman in the bed. *Okay, what in the world?* I shut the door and walk to the back bedroom, our bedroom, and when I open that door, I see two more naked people, but this time I recognize one of them: Jason's older sister, Pam. I turn around, pick up the phone, call Jason, and FREAK OUT. What is happening? I find out later that Pam is prostituting herself in our trailer while we're at school and work.

This was life, and it felt trashy and gross and I wanted out.

Jason cheats on me, which is terrible in the moment but great in the long run, because if he didn't, I may be tempted to stay with him just for the familiarity of it. I have no reason to stay in Georgia anymore. I'm ready to wipe the dust of that small town off my feet and start over. I don't want to be the trailer girl, the poor girl, the pregnant girl, the girl with the mom who is an alcoholic. I want to be a normal teenager. For me, Georgia means small-town hicks, trailers, poor education, school fights, racism, and neglect. It's depressing. I hate that I am the trailer-trash once-pregnant teen who hangs out with the poor boy with the crack-addicted mom. Georgia means trash. It means less-than. I feel *below*. Pennsylvania to me represents money and education and *better-than*. I feel above those in Georgia. In Pennsylvania, I have no reputation. I'm not trailer trash. I am normal, I am pretty, I am popular, and I feel above. Pennsylvania could be my new identity. I will be better than those who live in trailers and get pregnant as teens. I will be better and date a guy with normal parents. I will stay away from the kids who do drugs. I will stick with safe, stable, reliable, rich, cool. *I will never go back.*

He Bound Up
My Wounds

CHAPTER 7

New Life

Back in Pennsylvania, my dad's credit card is in my wallet and I'm headed to the mall.

I'll be starting eleventh grade in a week and I've got $250 to spend. New school, new clothes, *new life*. Here, I get the chance to start fresh. No one knows about the trailer or the alcohol or the pregnancy. In Pennsylvania, *I'm a normal girl*.

I move back in with my dad because my grandmother Julie is sick.

At home, my stepmom still isn't talking to me. But one morning, as I'm getting ready for school, she confronts me and tells me in a deep, angry voice that she will *never* forgive me. I tell her that God forgives me, even though I know nothing really of God . . . they're just words I say because I don't know what else to say.

"God may forgive you, but I don't."

Two moms—a stepmom and a biological mom—and I feel like I don't have a mom at all. But it's fine, because I have a good dad and I will be better and I will prove to her and myself and everyone else that I'm a *good girl*. It might be tense here, awful really, but it's still better than living with my mom. Plus, I'm used to the tightening in my stomach by now. I can live tense.

I start school and I'm the shiny new toy again, the new girl, and I attract attention. I reconnect with old friends, people who seem like normal teenagers, and I'm happy. I follow the crowd to Wednesday night Young Life where kids go to get out of the house on a school night. At Young Life we sing fun songs, watch adults make fools of themselves in skits, play games, and then hear a short message about Jesus. *I'm still trying to figure Jesus out.* I think He's God's Son or something?

In the fall I go to a Young Life weekend retreat where I see a boy who looks just like my movie-star crush, Jonathan Brandis. In between meetings, we hang out, and after the retreat we become a couple. He's older than me, a senior, and I begin to do the thing that scares most guys away: I start to act like we're married. Like, *immediately*. I'm *that* girl, because I'm insecure and want to be wanted *for real*.

He doesn't run away, but I find out later that it's because he heard I was easy. Which I was not, *at least I didn't think I was*. What was easy? Didn't all high school girls have sex? Apparently not, not in our high school anyway, and not in the eleventh grade. I remember being shocked when one guy I dated told me he hadn't had sex yet, and he was seventeen. *Shocked.* I didn't think people like him existed. And as for the whole "wait-for-marriage" thing, I had never heard of that *in my life*. The extent of my parental sex-talks were either my mom telling me about her own sex life or my dad telling me to have good morals. K, then.

Well Jonathan Brandis look-alike guy is smooth; he knows how to make moves and make me feel special, even if his motive is questionable. One night after work I get into my car, look up into my rear-view mirror, and there he is, JBLA (Jonathan Brandis Look Alike). He has a rose in his hand and looks all swoony. I get out of the car and run right into him, arms wrapping around him like I'm Gumby, and smiling like an idiot. We walk over to my car and get in. He looks at me with his big, blue JBLA eyes and kisses me. It's our first kiss. *This is sweet. This is real. He's not trying to—*

He sticks his tongue in my mouth and grabs my chest. Maybe my mom was right when she told me guys only wanted one thing. Seems so.

But he doesn't have a crack-addicted mom (his parents were together), he's a Christian (I think this means he's "good guy"), and he's cute. Surely he likes me for me, so I go for it. This is just how guys are. This is just how *I* am.

On another night in another car (his), I tell him about my abortion. I guess I have to get the secret out because it just sits on the lining of my soul waiting for me to come and get it and touch it and look at it and maybe think about it. I write poetry instead; when sadness covers me, I write. *I feel sad a lot.*

So I tell him, and I bawl like a baby, and he comforts me. It's genuine, I think. He gives me the bracelet on his wrist, a What Would Jesus Do one. I wear it for months.

What Would Jesus Do?

I like the phrase. I like it because it makes me think of Jesus, and I'm learning more about Him each Wednesday night. And at the retreat, when I wasn't crushing on JBLA, I was listening to the story of the man-God who went to a cross to die for me and for all my sins—past, present, and future—who defeated death, and who *knew* me and took for me all the bad things I had done. I was intrigued at that retreat, at this Jesus. I don't fully get it, but I want to know more, so I keep going to Young Life.

I keep going, I keep listening, and I'm given a New Testament, which, apparently, is a part of the Bible about Jesus. Sometimes I read it, and sometimes I even understand it. I want this, I want to be a Christian because I know Jesus is real and that He has called to me in the deep places of my soul. I'm still learning what it all means, but I am compelled to seek Him as He seeks me. I don't resist.

———

Sometimes I talk to my mom on the phone. We don't talk often.

———

I don't want to have sex anymore.

Apparently, there are guys (and girls) who choose to wait to have sex until they are married. There are GUYS who choose to wait. I thought guys only wanted one thing? Now I'm learning there are guys who are willing to get to know you first, to treat you kindly and with respect and honor you?

My boyfriend, JBLA, likes to look at naked women and it drives me nuts, but he says he's a Christian and he makes me feel like a jealous crazy person that I care. I'm not supposed to care; I've learned that. I learned years ago that my body is what gets me love—it's what gets me to be *not alone*. But now I look at the married Young Life leaders, and their marriages look different from what I've seen. I see affection and tenderness. I want that one day. Now that I know I don't have to have sex, I don't want to. I want to wait until someone will commit to me in marriage. And I'm not crazy for wanting that.

JBLA says he's fine with it, but then why is he still groping me?

I guess it's hard to stop once you've started. We try and fail and try and fail. I feel sick every time. Sometimes I cry, and this just gets on his nerves. I hate this. I hate doing what I don't want to do. "I do not understand what I do. For what I want to do I do not do, but what I hate I do" (Rom. 7:15 NIV).

———

JBLA goes to the local college and I start my senior year of high school. Every day on the drive home from school I tune into a new show I found called *The Dr. Laura Show*. I'm hooked. This Dr. Laura woman is all about rules and consequences and behavior, and I'm drawn to it all because I have lived so much chaos that seemed to be a consequence of not following the rules of *right* behavior. Moms shouldn't be alcoholics. Rules. Moms shouldn't be jerks to their kids and tell them they are stupid and ugly and treat them like they're worthless. Rules. Moms should love their kids and be home with them and give a crap about them and what they're doing. Rules, rules, rules. I read all of her books. I like her hard stances, I like her no-coddling way, I like that she called herself a "serious Jew." Well, since I am learning about Jesus and Christianity and I'm serious about it, I will now be called a "serious Christian." With rules you have control, and I'm desperate for control. I will be better. I will follow the rules in the Bible. I will be a good, serious, rule-following Christian. I will be in control of my life.

I barely understood grace before I jumped on the rule train. But this is the story, and this is the unfolding of it.

Mom's Journal | January 20, 2002 | I'm in college and Mom and I are struggling to maintain a relationship

Dear Lord,

Please forgive me for drinking a lot and being too late to go to church services to praise and honor You and for punishing myself for not being there. Please also forgive me for smoking so much and my fear of my job future. Thank You for being here in my loneliness. Help me to get with Your program, to do for You that which is why I am here.

CHAPTER 8

Surrender

I don't spend the summers with my mom now that I'm back with my dad. I'll visit for a week or so, but that's it, and I go mainly to see my sister.

Keitha is five years younger than me, and her dad is Mom's third husband. She is a blonde-haired beauty who resembles Britney Spears (although she hates that reference). Mom always calls Keitha the free-spirited child. I'm the uptight, too-serious one, the one who takes everything personally. Keitha, who Mom has taken to calling Summer, avoids all the emotional junk with Mom. She walled up young and decided to fend for herself when she didn't get the love and nurture from Mom. She was neglected and felt it deep and chose to bar whatever affection she had for Mom behind a steely exterior. For a short time while I was in Georgia she moved in with my grandparents (Poppy and Grandma) who also lived in Georgia, my mom's mom and dad. She told me that the years that she lived with them were the best years she had growing up. They cared for her, gave her boundaries and love and structure. They got her braces and helped her with her school work and she thrived. I don't know why I didn't move in with them, but it probably had to do with Jason and the freedom I had to do what I wanted. Also, I'm in an unhealthy attachment with Mom; I still think that if I just talk to her enough or explain myself, she'll understand, and we'll work things out. Of course, it's a delusion disguising as hope.

Mom and I can make it a few days together, either in person or on the phone, before she says something offensive to me and I go off on her and we both blow up. She has no edit; she says whatever she is thinking, and I am done being the little girl. I know how to leave now. Having a way out is a relief I'm grateful for.

My sister doesn't have it so easy. She's stuck, and one day she will tell me how she felt like I abandoned her when I moved back with my dad.

———

JBLA and I break up at the beginning of my freshman year at Penn State. It just so happened that I was in a Bible study with not one, but TWO girls he had cheated on me with. We all figured it out one night and let me tell you, *that* was something. The breakup is tougher than I thought it would be, but I know it's a good thing. Besides, I'm loving my freshman year of college. I love my classes (that don't start until 11:00 a.m.), my roommate is fun, and

I'm involved with a new ministry on campus that is all about leading students to a deeper relationship with Jesus. I join a Bible study, make friends, and am happy. *Except that I'm not.* When I'm alone, my insides crawl with anxiety.

I start skipping classes and stay in bed all day. My heart hurts, my body hurts, and I can't just get it together. What happened to my Dr. Laura sensibility? *Get up, girl, and get it together!* Slowly I drag myself back to life, going back to classes, telling my understanding professors that I've been depressed. (I'm a human development and family studies major so it's in their nature and profession to have sympathy for me.)

I decide, with a little convincing from my friends in the college ministry, to go out of town on their fall retreat. *I need to get away from here.* I wasn't going to go because I was still wallowing a bit in my sadness from JBLA, but with last-minute arrangements, I make the trip.

We have our first retreat session tonight, so I get my Bible and go to the main house to hear the speaker. I've been reading my Bible and scribbling notes in a notebook and I can't get enough. I'm learning so much and I think if only everyone knew that the words in the Bible are so good and so interesting and so wise and so relevant, they would read it and want to know more themselves. But I remember that I didn't always understand it, these words in verses, nor did I know what to read, where to start. It was as though I physically was unable to understand, like there was some kind of filter over my eyes and my heart. Until the wooing, the kind wooing of God that kept gently showing up, saying, "See? *Seek Me* and you will find Me. *Knock* on the door and it will be opened for you." I knocked, and it opened. My eyes opened, my heart opened, and I knew there was more; I knew there was a God and He called to me because He loved me.

I'm attuned to the retreat speaker and I'm ready to learn more about my God and the Jesus I'm still getting to know. He begins: "What would you do if Jesus walked into the room right now?" Well, that's a no-brainer. I'd hide. In fact, if Jesus walked in right now I would crawl over to that couch and hide behind it because Jesus wouldn't want to see me. To see me is to see inside me, and what is inside of me is filthy. I feel it. I feel it by the guilt and the dirt and the tight stomach and the "easy girl" past and the emptied womb. I feel it in my weakness and in how pitiful I am, how dumb I am. I hold a sparse amount of dignity, and even that I would give away to not be alone. No, Jesus would not want to see me, and quite frankly, I couldn't bear to see Him, I would feel it too much, the unworthiness attached to the ache to be loved.

After the talk is over I join my discussion group, and everyone seems to be cool with meeting Jesus in person. I'm asked what I would do, and I told them I would hide. I wish I could tell you what I'm hearing right now from the group members, but I can't, it's fuzzy. But what sticks, what takes root in my soul, is that I don't have to hide. Jesus knows everything about me and everything I've done, and He loves me. Still? Yes. "But God shows his love for us in that while we were still sinners, Christ died for us" (Rom. 5:8).

My life is not what makes or breaks Jesus' love for me; He loves me because He made me, and He wants me to know Him and to experience the depth of His love and the profound nature of His grace.

I see the pieces I've been trying to put together in this Jesus puzzle fall into place.

He made me. He sees right into me, knows it all, every scrap. "Even before a word is on my tongue, behold, O Lord, you know it altogether" (Ps. 139:4).

He loves me. And when I turn from Him and go my own way, escaping my pain with whatever my addiction, trying to fix the broken places with false fixtures, He comes for me. He did this by dying on a cross for my sins—my turning and my running and my fixing and the secret (and *not so* secret) choices toward darkness and ruin and ugliness—wearing it all, feeling it all, and destroying it all, and then rising up from it, defeating it for good. He has defeated the death that wants my soul. My sins are so far from me now in my God's eyes, they are as far as the east from the west. He remembers my sin no more. Gone. All of it—the stuff I did like having sex and lashing out and even the abortion, but also all the stuff done to me, like the neglect from my mom, the ways boys took advantage of my vulnerability, the abuse, and even my brokenness from it all and exhaustion from trying to be good—God has seen and paid for *all of it*. In my Father's eyes, I am righteous and clean and called "daughter." And that good root that Jesus planted in my soul, it's a vine, and that vine is wrapped up with me and I with it, with Him.

I chose to believe, to trust in what I can't see but what is infiltrating my very being.

Grace entered into me with a fullness that night that I didn't yet know, and truth surrounded me, and I surrendered all to Him. My life, my broken places, my wounded heart, and all that I have.

Mom's Journal | May 18, 2002 | I'm in college and the relationship with my mom is a constant struggle and I often think maybe I'll just walk away from her completely

What's going on with me and my girls? I don't know what they feel, think, are doing or not doing in their heads about me . . . not at all or just so not good that I'm left out . . . or is it their age? I don't think so . . . I'm feeling they have little respect for me, but I don't say anything . . . I must find ways to share with them . . . I'm not sure who they are as I've been in the past . . . what is my current role as mother? I'm losing out, left out, shut out.

I wish I could take back the many times I put my selfish ways ahead of my children when they were growing up . . . I wish I'd now have wonderful memories to recollect with them, special . . . I wish I'd been more of a mother and less out of control and needy. Bet my kids would look up to me if I were a better mother . . .

CHAPTER 9

Obnoxious Jesus Girl

I am now obnoxious Miss Jesus Girl.

This is what happens when you go from light to dark, blind to seeing—you want to tell everyone. You play the song "Jesus Freak" as loud as you can in your dorm and your poor roommate walks in and, shaking her head and rolling her eyes, promptly walks out.

You argue with an atheist college student in the evenings and get your Bible facts wrong and *he* corrects *you*. You've met Jesus in a deep-down personal, *blood-in-your-veins* kind of way, but you aren't skilled in Bible knowledge. *Yet.* You may or may not go into chat rooms and tell everyone about the locusts from Revelation. *You might be a new Christian if* . . . surely that's a punch line.

The thing is, the joy in the experience is so true and so good and so sweet, that many of us haven't learned the wisdom of hushing as we learn. Us newbie Christians who come to the table later are just so enthusiastic that we often act the fool. Bear with us. We'll eventually settle down and get quiet and humble, if we're teachable, and learn to listen more than we speak and serve more than we shout.

———

In the college ministry I meet Blake. He's tall and has these tender green eyes that pierce me. Blake is a Christian, but not a JBLA Christian. He's gentle and kind. He treats me with respect. We don't have sex (at least not until a couple years later when pain and longing and loneliness lead to sex because it seems like the only thing that might make us feel good enough for each other).

This is new. *This is good.*

But I'm a really clingy girlfriend. It's that whole *I don't want to be alone and I need you to want me forever right now* thing.

Blake and I break up and make up and make-out, and break up and make up.

I'm really, really trying to follow Jesus. I'm learning so much in my Bible studies and personal study times, and I even begin to lead Bible studies. I go to all the events the college ministry puts on, and I do my best to be good. *It will take years before I learn to stop all that trying.*

I visit my mom on Christmas breaks, and we do okay. I want her to know Jesus, and I want to forgive her and love her, so I keep going. I try, and I think she tries, but something always gets said and we fall apart all over again. I keep hoping something will change, that she'll stop drinking, that she'll act like a mother. Maybe I am too sensitive. Maybe she's just a wretched, cold-hearted, selfish, mean woman.

––––––

Blake and I spend our college years breaking up and making up. During a breakup, I get a new boyfriend, Matt. He's an artist and plays guitar, and around him I feel free. I love him. I make plans in my heart to be his forever. He eventually breaks up with me and I think my heart is broken for good.

I'm alone again. And this time I don't have a roommate. I live in an apartment by myself. My dad owns it, so it's free for me.

There it is again, the anxiety, the *crawling, anxious, slithering* thing that soon will have me at a bar or a party, finding someone to hold onto. *Why can't I just be a good girl? What is wrong with me?*

Mom's Journal | 2001| Mom is single and alone

I am lonely, and it is okay. I wish I had a good man by my side.

CHAPTER 10

Something Has to Change

Mom and I make plans to go to Myrtle Beach for a few days together. We just *keep on* with this relationship. I'm trying to be a *good* Christian and show her love. We'll get a hotel room and we'll eat all-you-can crab legs and enjoy the beach. We'll be careful not to step on any land mines with each other. I will not mention her drinking.

We keep our conversations shallow, and I make her laugh with my impersonations. I love making her laugh. *Maybe things will be different this time.* But inevitably, the butting heads begins. She gets angry with me for something, blames me, offers her calm comments ripe with barbs, and I try to defend myself, but it only leads to us in the car driving home and my once-settled rage is spiking. Every time I think the fire has died down, it flares. We pull over and I call my dad on a pay phone. My breathing is erratic, and

I can't dam up the onslaught of tears. "Dad, I can't take this, I can't take her, I hate her, I can't!"

My dad, with level-headed sensibility says, "You can't stay in the middle of the highway. You have to get in the car and deal with it for the ride and then come home."

I know he's right, but I don't want to be near her, trapped in a car with her venom. What choice is there? I get back in the car and she drives. Her poison is in me. She's cool as a cucumber. I'm the one who is wrong, unreasonable, *sensitive*. The angrier I get, the calmer she gets. Her self-righteousness is the air I'm breathing and it's suffocating me.

I can't wait to get away from her.

God, how am I supposed to do this?

————

It's like I never learn.

I go visit her again, *I try again*, but this time I take my boyfriend Matt with me (this is before he breaks up with me). Big mistake.

The first night we're there all sitting together—me, my sister, my mom, and Matt—and my mom starts making fun of me. She's laughing at my expense and she's drunk and I'm trying to start a new conversation, keep things cordial, but it's not happening. As usual, *I'm just too sensitive.*

It's the next day and I'm in mom's bathroom putting makeup on. Mom doesn't understand me, and I don't understand her. *My rage builds.* I feel alone;

I'm twenty-one years old but I feel like that weak little girl who used to live here. I start venting about my mom, trying to release some of the fire, and my boyfriend doesn't respond. All of a sudden, my rage directs at him. He's calm, *too calm*, like my mother. Why isn't he defending me? Why is he just sitting there, emotionless?

I'm not in the bathroom anymore. My hands are at his face, his body, and guttural cries are coming out of my mouth and my eyes and he tries to defend himself, but I just keep hitting him.

I finally stop, and my bones become like jelly.

The floor steadies my curled-up, heaving body.

When I can breathe again I sit up, gain composure, and write Mom a letter telling her I need to stay away for a while. I take the blame because I know leaving will hurt her. I am as nice as I can be. I leave the note on the dining room table and get the heck out of Dodge.

The Letter

> Mom,
>
> First of all, I want you to know that I love you very much. As hard as it is, I need to accept your drinking because you tell me that it is who you are. I don't believe it is, but I am not in your shoes and have no place to judge. I do feel, however, that

you can get very mean sometimes and it makes me not want to be around you. I don't want to lose you as my mom, but I just don't know what to do. I feel like I have to leave early to gather my thoughts about how to be a kind and loving daughter.

As of now, I don't seem to be doing a very good job of showing you Christ's love through me, and that makes me realize I need to take a good look in the mirror at who I am and work harder at becoming the person God intended me to be. I think I blame a lot of your personality on your drinking, but that's only because I find it so hard to believe that some of the things that come out of your mouth are from a mother. "Whatever," "[expletive]," and talking about me not forgiving you for what happened with the pregnancy. That is the past and it has been forgiven, and I hope you know that God has forgiven you. I've never blamed you; I just want you to know that. It really hurt when you talked about that though, but I know you said you're sorry, and I accept it. I hope you can accept my apology for my attitude and my behavior. I really do care about you; I really just need to pray about this. Anyway, I'm sorry I hurt you, I really am.

Love always, Sarah Mae

Mom's Journal | 2001 | Visions on Sarah

I'm going to let go of her, pray that God watches over her in my absence. Thoughts of her recent behavior make me angry, depressed, extremely sad, and I hate to say it, but provides too good an opportunity for the devil to rule. It is wrong for her to treat her mother this way, so I've decided not to give much thought to this situation she has created between us. Her intentions are not good.

CHAPTER 11

Core Lies

Today I am getting together with Cathy Bowman, the campus minister's wife. She is a wise and kind woman, a mentor, who has a sign in her bathroom that says, "The Lord is with you wherever you go."

Her home is cozy, and her woodstove is burning with an aroma that makes you want winter all year long. She offers me tea. We sit at her dining room table and I tell her that I don't know what is wrong with me, but I'm a mess. She listens as I talk and then she pulls out a yellow notepad.

She faces it toward me and writes these words:

> I am bad
> I am shameful
> I am forgettable
> I am not in control
> I am ugly

I am stupid
I am wrong
I am a failure
I am defective
I am lazy
I am not good enough

As she's writing, she asks me if any of these things stand out to me or hit my heart. Several do, but two of them were most prominent: I am not in control and I am not good enough. She circles them.

Next, she writes this:

I must be good enough (perfectionist)
I must be in control
I must be fit
I must be smart
I must be pretty
I must be right
I must be successful
I must be wanted
I must hide myself

She asks me to circle the ones that hit me.

I must be good enough. I must be smart.

She explains to me that these beliefs, these "core lies," are what we believe deep down about ourselves, in our core. She explains that God has given us longings to be loved and to make an impact, but that we live in a fallen world where we have hurtful and painful experiences, and because we are thinkers, we come up with conclusions.

"You know how children are great observers but terrible interpreters?"

I nod.

She continues by telling me that we come up with lies about the world and ourselves and God and others based on our childhood observations. And then, unconsciously, we form these goals that become demands. Usually these goals aren't bad at first, but it's when we make them demands that they become disastrous. This affects our behaviors. We become manipulative and self-protective, and it shows up in our emotions with anger, anxiety, and depression.

She draws me a little chart that looks like this:

> Anger = a blocked goal
> Anxiety = uncertain if we can accom-
> plish our goal
> Depression = an unattainable goal (this
> is different from clinical depression)

As she's explaining these things, I'm starting to think, if there are reasons for why I feel and act crazy, maybe something can be done about it. If I know the truth, *the why*, maybe I can be set free.

My mind is spinning,

"What's the lie?"

She says that the lie is the belief and what's *attached* to the belief.

I look at the yellow notepad. *I'm not good enough.* This belief translates into me needing to be smart and taken seriously. I must be smart; I must be taken seriously. When someone doesn't take me seriously, I freak out. Because if I'm not taken seriously, then you're saying I'm not good enough, worthy enough, to be taken seriously. At the end of it, you're saying that I don't matter. *You are acting like my mom who laughed at me when I told her how much she hurt me.* The lie is that my worth and value are determined if I'm smart or if others take me seriously. It's also a lie that I can manipulate and control my world to avoid being hurt.

Oh my goodness. I've been living out of my lies. But I don't have to anymore, I can name them and then I can believe the truth.

Cathy draws on the yellow notepad again. This time she draws a circle and she asks me, "What is it that we all want?" *We all want to be loved and secure.*

She says the great thing about recognizing our core lies is that it forces us to go the gospel of good news: that Jesus Christ paid with His life for all our past, present, and future sins, and I do not have to be whatever these lies are. Our worth and value is *only* dependent on how Christ sees us, and He sees us as righteous. He loves us. We are secure in Him.

I don't have to be good enough or smart enough or even taken seriously by others. How they view me does not determine my worth, only Jesus determines my worth.

Game changer.

I know there's still so much work to be done here, more lies to uncover, but now that I know, now that I see this new thing, I can continue in the truth.

For too long I have beat myself up for not being able to get myself together, to fix myself, for not being able to control my emotions. I have hated myself for being so weak, so emotional, so easily affected. I don't want to do this to myself anymore. I want to be free.

I thank Cathy for teaching me about core lies. She doesn't know it at the time, but she would be the first of many wise counselors in my life whom God sent to help me process the complicated nature of my life and my faith.

She rips the yellow page off the notepad and gives it to me. I treasure it. I hug her goodbye and walk out of her house with a newfound sense of freedom.

Mom's Journal | October 2001 | Mom and I are at a loss with each other

Dear Jesus,

I am so confused. I am so blessed in Your presence, to feel Your love, to know I am to love others first and foremost. Yet, today I had no patience, and spoke ill of others once again, even knowing it was wrong. Please forgive me. I can't stand the way I feel—like I'm never going to get it together, over and over behaving outside of Your ways that mean life to me. The only time I feel alive is when I'm basking in Your Light; I know my faith and my strength are in You. Am I ever going to be able to show my children the love they need from their mother? Please forgive me these questions. I want so much to give out love. Instead, I keep tripping over myself, frustrated, me getting in the way of progress.

Dear Lord, I love You. Please forgive me. Please take away that part of me that gets in the way, that part of me that distorts love, and life. The part that despises me for my failures, that part which is not love. Please take it away from me or carry me until it is gone. Forgive me my weaknesses, help me to reside in Your strength, and give to others as You have given to me for I know You are there and able to comfort.

CHAPTER 12

Holding the Ball

It's my junior year of college and I'm sitting in my favorite class, preparing to continue learning all about family dynamics and abuse and relationships. It's what we've been studying lately, and it's right up my ally. Basically, my college classes are like therapy.

I settle in my seat for more information about dysfunctional families when a bald man with a dark mustache and black leather jacket walks to the front of the class. We have a guest lecturer today. He's some kind of drug and alcohol counselor.

My body straightens and my head leans forward. *Tell me what you know, Bald Man, because I need what you know.* He lectures for forty-five minutes on substance abuse and how it affects families, and all I really care about is grabbing him after class and telling him about my mom and asking him what to do with my mom and our jacked-up relationship.

The minute we are dismissed, I move through the desks, bumping my hips in my hurry, and run down the steps toward the door where he's standing. I ask him if I can talk to him for a few minutes. He says yes.

I tell him about my mom. I tell him that she drinks sunup to sundown and that she knows she's an alcoholic but doesn't care. I tell him how, when I'm around her, I feel crazy rage sliding under the surface, but that I'm also helpless to help her, to make her happy. I can never say the right things or do the right things; I feel guilty around her; I disappoint her. And she tells me so. I tell him that we are so tangled up with each other that I don't know what is true and what isn't. Am I just too sensitive? What do I do?

"Don't throw the ball back."

I scrunch my face at him. "Huh?"

"If I have a ball in my hand and I throw it to you, are you going to catch it?"

"Yeah, I guess."

"Okay," he says, "well, you made that choice; you caught the ball. Now you have another choice to make: you can hold the ball, drop the ball, or throw the ball back." He tells me this ball-throwing situation is what is going on with my mom. He says we are engaged in a game of toss. She throws out a ball of verbal abuse or manipulation (this is a new word for me), and I always respond by throwing the ball back; I engage with her. "Mom, I tried, I really did. I don't know what you want me to do!" (Ball toss.) "Sarah, if you would have just . . ." (Ball toss.) "Mom, you're really hurting my feelings . . . why do you have to be like this?" (Ball toss.) "Get a grip, Sarah, you are way too sensitive." (Ball toss.)

On and on, back and forth, a seemingly never-ending game.

"If you don't want to play the game anymore, *stop throwing the ball back.*"

If she calls and starts being verbally abusive to me or manipulating me, I can hang up the phone. I can start by saying, "If you keep talking to me like this, I'm going to hang up." But often that doesn't work because the person will suck you in with explanations and manipulations and it just stays messy and the call drags on and the ball stays in play.

Bald Man says I can make an excuse: "Sorry, Mom, gotta go, someone's at the door." Click. Or I can just say, "Gotta go," and hang up before she responds. What I don't want to do is stay in the spiral. If I don't hang up she'll keep talking, keep pushing. Ending our conversation abruptly seems rude and harsh, and it is, but it's a boundary that will save my sanity.

I feel a responsibility to make things right with her, but I'm being ineffective because I am trapped in unhealthy behaviors and tangled thinking.

I'm an emotionally unhealthy person trying to help an emotionally unhealthy person.

And it isn't working. Of course.

Today I will stop throwing the ball. *God help me.*

———

I do it. I stop throwing the ball back when we're on the phone. I tell her I will no longer stay on the phone with her if she is unkind to me. My mom hates when I hang up, but it's my only way out, and I need out. I'm learning so much about my own emotions and false beliefs, and now, how to set boundaries.

I'm on a learning high. I want to know all the things. I want to learn more about setting boundaries. I get a copy of the book *Boundaries* by Henry Cloud and John Townsend.

I learn that, "Made in the image of God, we were created to take responsibility for certain tasks. Part of taking responsibility, or ownership, is knowing what *is* our job, and what *isn't*. . . . Any confusion of responsibility and ownership in our lives is a problem of boundaries."[3]

It is not my job to fix my mom.

My job is to trust God, obey where He leads, and become spiritually and emotionally healthy *so that* I can love others, including my mom. And I know God wants me to love my mom because He won't let me let go of her. But He doesn't want me to be messed up, tangled up, manipulated, or abused. Okay, *so one step at a time.*

I learn that *boundaries are not walls.* Boundaries are more like fences with gates, allowing the good in and keeping the bad out. "The most basic boundary-setting word is *no* . . . we can set limits on our own exposure to people who are behaving poorly; we can't change them or make them behave right."[4]

This is what Bald Man taught with the ball. "No, Mom, you may not speak to me that way. If you do, I will have to hang up/leave."

I realize that I need to do more than just hang up. I need time to clear my head and get my thoughts right. I've been confused and tangled up for so long. I make the decision to take six months "off" from Mom. I'm not going to talk to her or see her.

Mom's Journal | 2001| After deciding
I needed time away from her

I'm down, it feels like for the count since Sarah's rejection so very rudely put before me on her last visit, the winds of my sail have not been blowing. Although my faith in Jesus keeps me afloat, my identification with this, my first-born child, is now without a link to me. She sums up all of me as drinking; nothing else, just my drinking. That is her reason, besides me hurting her, all racked up to me and my drink. If ever before there were anyone who seemed to understand the pains of my upbringing, and the shortcomings because of that as a part of me, I have always thought it would be Sarah.

She was the only one who listened, and I thought understood, and was willing to forgive my faults, and love me besides, and who I thought knew I loved her the best I could. Now she is gone, removed herself from my life, confessing a distaste for association with me, disgustingly asserting she loves me, at the same time asserting I hurt her too much to associate with me. Perhaps some time in the future, she says.

Never would I have suspected that Sarah, all the while making me believe she honestly cared, understood, respected, accepted, and proud to be my daughter, quoting that some of her best qualities as a Christian, came from the values I taught her growing up, were lies. All she wants me to do is stop drinking; all my flaws she's racked up as my drinking. God, I wish that all I'd have to do is stop drinking and all my bills would be paid and I'd not have to work like a dog to survive, that all the love I feel for my children would flow like a geyser, and I would the mother I always wanted to be for them, and the world would open to me in all the ways I've always wanted . . . then, she'd have no reason to reject me, to lie and say she loves me. She is blind to my pain, now, from my past, and my present. She is blind to my struggles and the goodness of my intentions. She has deserted me, left me more alone than I ever was, and she doesn't even know.

I was once proud. Her arrogance, judgmentalness, better-than-me, fake, lying self hurts me to the bone. Her listening and standing up for me wasn't real . . . wasn't real . . . wasn't real.

I am no longer a part of her life. I must accept that it is reality, and I have always hated reality, and with good cause. Sarah now makes me feel that I would be good to her if I were dead; then I'd be the mother she could make believe . . . I'd have to be dead first . . . be dead . . . oh, God, my pain increases. Please forgive me, my pain increases.

CHAPTER 13

Mourning the Loss of a Mother

Now that I'm not talking to my mom, a new pain surfaces.

I want a mom. I don't have a mom. *God, it hurts.*

I scribble some unedited thoughts in a notebook:

> *What's it like?*
> *What's it like to be held by her?*
> *What's it like to cry on her shoulder?*
> *What's it like to come home to some-*
> *   one who wants to hear about your*
> *   day?*
> *What's it like to talk to her about boys?*
> *What's it like to ask her for advice?*
> *What's it feel like when she hugs you?*
> *What's it like to need her?*
> *What's it like to be loved by her?*

What's it like?
I never had her, but I miss her so much.

My desire for a mom is intensifying, and there seems to be a gaping hole where the love of a mother is supposed to be.

It's interesting because after learning about core lies and how I've self-protected for so long, I wasn't prepared for the emotions that would come when I laid down my self-protection. Turns out, under all the self-protecting, I'm really sad about not having a mother.

I've gone so long without motherly affection that I guess I thought I was fine without it. *I'm not.* I see other daughters with their moms and they're happy. Their moms might not be perfect, but they let their daughters cuddle up next to them and put their head on their mom's shoulder. The daughters ask their moms for advice and they talk about what's on their mind, their joys and their heartaches. Their moms defend them, and protect them, and nurture them, and they *know* they are loved. I'm so jealous. I hate them all. I don't really, *but I kind of do.*

I believe that Mom loves me somewhere in her heart, in her own way, in the way she is capable, I guess. But she does not love me the way my heart desires it, the way a daughter's heart is designed for a mother's love. There is a crevice in my heart that she isn't filling, like a cavity that irritates the gums and grows bigger and deeper if not treated; I feel it. But I don't know how to fix it.

I need to talk to someone about this pain.

The church I attend gives me a recommendation for a counselor. This is how I meet Melanie.

I take myself and my *mother issues* to this Melanie woman, and we sit down in her small office and I smile nervously because *maybe this is dumb that I'm here*. We make small talk, *blah blah blah*, and at some point, I tell her my mom didn't send me a birthday card this year, and I know it's dumb, but I'm really sad about it.

We talk, and by "we" I mean "me," and it turns out there is a load of sorrow and despondency right underneath my skin. I'm flat-out sad, down to the bone, cry-me-a-river, *sad*. And also, I'm pretty ticked off. My mom abandoned her role as mother, and she chose her alcohol over her children and she is a mean, offensive, unedited, stubborn, *word I will not use here*. And another also, I want to be held. Will I ever have a mother like that, like the kind that holds their daughters and carries their hearts? That's mushy, *I know*, but this is where I'm at. Mush and ache and anger and desperate for physical affection.

Here is what I *want* to hear Melanie tell me: Yes, it's possible to have those things, maybe not with your mom, but maybe another woman will fill that role. Maybe another woman will adopt you as her own and take you in and nurture you and give you *all* that your heart has been longing for. Melanie did not say those words. Instead she said this:

"You have to mourn the loss of a mother."

I don't know how long I stared at Melanie before the tears tumbled out. I would have to release her as my mom, grieve her as though she died. Because the reality is, *I don't have her.* I don't have the mom my daughter heart longs for. Waiting for her to be something she's not is just keeping the wound open. It's time to begin to let it heal.

I feel like my insides are being ripped out.

———

We have to mourn because it is the process of *accepting reality*.

And how do we accept reality? Here's what Melanie tells me:

We Acknowledge It

The worst thing we can do is dam up our feelings. When we have trauma, when bad things happen, and we have to function, sometimes we compartmentalize. We don't deal with it, we stuff it down and wall up. Doing this separates us from our emotions. We stuff through denial, busyness, all sorts of ways. When we do this, when we stuff it down, eventually our stuffing begins to develop cracks and emotions come out. We try to put fingers in the holes, but that inevitably breaks, and many times in ways we don't like. Some people bottle up their whole lives and live half-dead. This quote (often attributed to Ben Franklin but not sourced) says it best: "A man dies at 24 and is buried at 64." We develop anxiety in feeling our emotions and we try to control life so we don't have to feel them.

Anxiety says, "I can't handle it." The truth is, whatever the pain, it won't destroy us, and "this too shall pass." If we really can't handle it, that's when we should seek out a counselor.

Everyone Is Different

What works for me might not work for you. You have to figure out what brings release and healing to your own heart. Some people process by sitting and crying, talking to friends and family, some through journaling, doing art, running, music, and so on. There are a variety of ways. One thing that's important regardless: use the things that bring you peace and joy to help you process your feelings.

She gives me some examples: If you're a beach person, you could get some stones and for every stone you throw into the ocean you say, "I'm so sad about _____ and wish you were _____."

Or if you paint, paint a portrait of loss. If you write, write out your pain.

Take Time

Two weeks after a loss is usually when the crash happens. This is why community and funerals are so important. Anything you can unload off your plate during this time is wise. Call friends to help you. Understand that people want to know how to help. When emotions come up, *feel them*, observe them, let them *naturally* dissipate. Be honest in processing reality. "Lord, is there something You want to say to me about this?" (My friend Amy said her mom's friend says, "Come here, pain. What do you want to teach me?")

For some of us, the crash happens five, fifteen, twenty years into the unresolved grief. The same thing holds true: Be honest. Let the pain do its work. Let the feelings come. The important thing is not stuffing it, but vulnerably facing it and walking through it. *The healing comes through the pain.*

If You're in a Strained Relationship

First, ask yourself: What should my expectations actually be, and in what ways am I putting myself, relationship, or other person into a state of continual failure? For example, I keep expecting my mom to be a mother, because she should be one, but the fact is, she isn't. The expectation is unrealistic, and all it's doing is causing more hurt for me and a state of failure for her, because she can't be what I want her to be.

Second, fight to let go of these faulty expectations. Once you do, it opens the door to seeing the person as a person, as who they really are *as a person*. This makes us more compassionate. Again, with my mom, as I let go of the expectation that she will *mother* me, I will be able to see her as a human who is flawed and in need of love, just like me. I can't look to her anymore to give me what I need from a mother. I need to release her and my expectation. Is this going to be easy? No, it's gutting, and it will take time, but ultimately, it's the most healthy thing I can do because it's real. *Mourning/grieving is the process of facing reality.*

If you're in a toxic situation or an abusive one, you need to figure out what you are or are not willing to tolerate. This happens through a *lot* of personal prayer, and a *lot* of input from healthy community and counselors around you who 1) know you well; 2) aren't tangled up in the crazy the way you are and thus have better judgment on what is tolerable and what is absolutely not tolerable; and 3) are committed to helping you fight the tendency to do this work of boundaries and healing in isolation. The key to all of this is to stay tender to the Lord's leading in all of it. Each relationship and every decision on boundaries is just so personal.

Third, learn contentment with not having a need met. Yes, having unmet needs will hurt deeply.

But even in the pain, this is still true: I can have a fulfilling, loving life even if some of my needs won't be met. I hurt that I don't have a mom, but I have a good life. No person on earth has all needs met at all times.

Fourth, when anxiety prevents you from grieving, when you think you can't handle it, accept *in faith* that God is going to take care of you. You're not going to wither unless you act in a sabotaging way.

Fifth, pray and remember Philippians 4:6–7: "Do not be anxious about anything, but in everything by prayer and supplication with thanksgiving let your requests be made known to God. And the peace of God, which surpasses all understanding, will guard your hearts and your minds in Christ Jesus." You might feel anxious, but you don't have to *do* anxious. You can offer the anxiety—the feelings, the sleepless nights, the weight of it—up to God who will give you peace through a variety of creative ways. Be open to His leading.

Is God Enough?

I had one more question for Melanie:

"Is God enough?"

"Sarah, that question is thinking of God in a narrow way. When I ask that question, it's like I'm isolating myself from wanting or needing anything from friends or life. If God can talk through a donkey (Num. 22:28), He can speak to you in a variety of ways. He is creative enough to meet your needs and be with you in a variety of ways that speak to the needs *He knows* are the most important for you to have fulfilled."

"And Sarah?"

"Yes?"

"It's okay that we will always have a little bit of sadness in our life regarding loss. The goal isn't to never be sad, it's about getting to the point where the pain no longer *consumes* us or *controls* our perceptions of ourselves, others, God, and the world.

"When we let go of our faulty expectations of others and our habit of shoving people into roles that we need them to fulfill, and instead accept them for who they really are, it opens a door to having a lot more peace and happier relationships that are about *here and now.*

"Forgive your mom for not being what she should have been."

Mom's Journal | 1989

I want my mommy. I want my unconditional love, now, mommy, please.

CHAPTER 14

Caked-on Face

I feel like I'm in the land of the wounded. I've been learning so much, but all this learning just seems to be opening up more wounds.

I'm still seeing Melanie and learning to walk in this new grief, this new acknowledgment that I don't have a mom. My heart is so tender these days, *fragile*.

I begin dating Blake again.

In a session with Melanie I tell her that I'm dating Blake again, and how I've been feeling guilty because when we were first together my freshman year, I got drunk at a party and had sex with someone else. I've never told him, and it's kind of eating away at me.

She tells me I need to tell him.

She's lost her mind. It was freshman year! It's in the past.

"I can't tell him—he'll break up with me."

She says he might, but he needs to know the truth. She also tells me that if I want to change, if I don't want to make the same mistakes again, I have to face the consequences of my sin. There's a tightening in my stomach. *Am I going to throw up?* Okay. I'll tell him. I want to be free from the secret and the guilt. And she's right, he needs to know the truth.

God help me. I want to do the right thing. I want nothing to hinder me from knowing and following You with my whole heart.

Blake and I are in his room. "I have to tell you something, and it's bad, but I need you to listen."

His eyes are on mine. He says okay.

My mouth arches into a smile so I take a pillow and cover my face. *I hate that I laugh when I'm nervous.* Through the pillow I tell Blake about the party and what happened, how I slept with someone after drinking too much. Once it's clear that I was a willing participant that night, that I did indeed cheat on him, he told me to leave.

Is this a breakup? I don't know. But I did it, I said it, and now we both know, and we are both free.

After some time, he actually forgives me.

But then, on a lonely, anxiety-driven night when Blake isn't around, I do it again. I sleep with someone else, and I'm not drunk, just lonely.

I tell Blake, *again*, what I did. He walks to the door, opens it, and says, "You're just like your mother and you will never change. Get out."

I jump at the echo of the door hitting the latch.

I am not just like my mother. *I will change.*

———

Tortured soul full of disgrace
That can't replace
or erase
The sin that lies within
A divorce it is that reeks with pain and
guilt and shame
That hides behind the game
You used to hug me so tight
It's as if you thought you could squeeze
the hurt and destruction out
Now all you want to do is shout
I felt as though my caked-on face was
getting harder to remove
So sad and tired and limp
I was afraid it was becoming my own
My body on loan
Now I live with the consequences of my
selfish actions
Taking in
Deserving your reactions
Sorrys are pathetic and explanations are
a slap in the face
So I sit with my tortured soul
Full of disgrace

My caked-on face. My body on loan. Enough alcohol to numb my senses.

Disgraced.

Maybe I am just like my mom.

God help me.

———

I'm twenty-two years old and I'm in my dad's office. In his desk I find a report about me from kindergarten. The swirly letters on the page indicate that I acted "inappropriately" and showed sexual affection to other students. I am told I was put into counseling for my "odd behaviors."

I asked my mom if she had any knowledge of me being sexually abused as a child. She tells me she doesn't. The counselor from my childhood tells me she believes I witnessed my mom having sex, and that's why I was the way I was. No one really knows anything, and it's the not knowing why I am the way I am that is so frustrating. I know I'm a sinner, but why this sin, this way?

My mom talked to me about sex early and openly. When I was ten she brought home a man and told me to stay downstairs with his son. We sat on the couch, staring at nothing, waiting. I wanted him to make a move on me. I leaned across him to turn off the light, hoping to entice him. Nothing.

The next day mom told me she only slept with the guy for his body.

I learned at a young age that sex was power. I learned it from my mom, from the old British man who stuck his tongue in my twelve-year-old mouth at a get-together (there wasn't enough soap that could wash away the filth), from Shawn (the ex-stepbrother), and from various guys along the way. I was equally confused and fascinated by this power.

I learned something else as well: that I, Sarah, could be separate from my body. I don't know the first time I learned this lesson, but I do remember a day when it was reinforced. It was years ago, before coming to faith and before Cathy and before Melanie, when I was fourteen and had gotten drunk with Jason, the first boyfriend. On a walk home, through a field that for some reason had a bench in it, we sat down. I'm pretty sure we had been drinking because I remember pretending to be passed out, and that it was plausible that he would believe it. I did this just to see what he would do. He began to have sex with me. I was completely uninvolved, passive, tired, drunk, but he did it anyway. I didn't have to be involved, which meant *I* didn't hold the power, my body did.

I had another boyfriend who did the same thing after I drank too much. I wasn't involved, but just let it happen. In the same moment I thought I was testing out a theory, I was actually being abused and had no idea. At that point in my life, it never struck me as wrong for me to impair my own judgment, or for a guy to take physical advantage of a girl who was drunk. I was being sinned against and I was also a sinner in the same moment somehow. On that bench, when a guy was being twisted with me, I also had a twisted curiosity about the whole thing, about the fact that guys would do what they wanted to me even when I wasn't involved.

There was me, my personhood, and there was my body, and I thought I could separate the two. I believed that I had no power, but my body, separate from me, did. It was the thing guys wanted, I just happened to come along with it. *I didn't understand then that the body and the soul are intimately linked, and what happens to the body happens to the soul. There is no separation.*

So I let my body get me what I wanted and felt so deprived of: closeness, love, the illusion of security. If I gave my body, then I wasn't alone. I could be close to another person, and that person would want me. I would be worthy of attention and affection and love. I would be wanted.

Sex became a deterrent to loneliness and a power worth having. Sex was never intimate or special or sacred or good. It was a tool, a *means*. And that's what I used it for. Even now, as I'm in my junior year of college and trying to follow Jesus, it's what I use when I'm in pain. I find someone to be with because it's the only way to not feel the pain. It's the only way to escape the loneliness and the depression and the confusing darkness.

I don't want to do this. I know better and want to be better, but need wins over my determination to stop. *The need is stronger than the conviction.* So I find refuge wrapped with another body.

———

I hate this. *What is wrong with me? Why can't I just stop?* My eyes can't adjust to this darkness. The pit is deep and I'm not sure light can get in. My bones are barely holding up my flesh.

God, I can't go any lower. If You don't do something, I'm not going to make it.

I waited patiently for the LORD;
he inclined to me and heard my cry.
He drew me up from the pit of
destruction,
out of the miry bog,
and set my feet upon a rock,
making my steps secure.
He put a new song in my mouth,
a song of praise to our God.
Many will see and fear,
and put their trust in the LORD.
(Ps. 40:1–3)

CHAPTER 15

He Heals the Brokenhearted

The door sticks, so I pull harder and stumble back. The dark-brown door is open, and I walk through.

I'm here at this counseling office because I need an internship for my major, and this place is only two blocks from my apartment. I'm not sure what kind of counseling place this is, but I ask for an application anyway. Scanning the questions, I pause on one: What do you know about abortion? *That's a weird question.*

After a quick drive I pull into Barnes & Noble and surprisingly find a book on abortion called *Forbidden Grief: The Unspoken Pain of Abortion.* I want to have a good answer for the question on the application, so I buy the book and take myself to a coffee shop to read it.

An hour later I'm picking through wet tissues, trying to find a dry one to handle the rest of this mess coming out of me.

I learn that many women who have had abortions often exhibit a variety of destructive behaviors, escape in forms of alcohol, drugs, sex . . .

They experience depression, suicidal thoughts, and even have post-traumatic stress.

I read about the trauma and the destruction and the ache and I see that some of my pain has to do with my abortion. Of course it does.

I'm not alone. I'm not crazy. Other women who have had abortions have been in the pit just like I have been.

I know what I need to do.

———

I'm standing in front of the dark door that sticks.

Pushing my feet forward, one step, two, I walk into the lobby. *You can do this.* A woman sees me, and I try to look into her eyes, but the little girl is making an appearance. I'm small. But I know I'm where I'm supposed to be; I know that God in His kindness has led me here to heal my broken heart and bind up some wounded places. "I came here for a job, but I think the Lord wants me to deal with my abortion."

———

Ann, my post-abortion counselor, and I spend six weeks together going through a Bible study called

Forgiven and Set Free. She's safe, and with her I am able to express all the emotions I'd locked up. I knew I was depressed, but I didn't know just how angry I was, or how under all that anger was sadness and confusion and serious detachment.

In between counseling sessions I write in my journal:

> I am so frustrated. I'm trying to get through this whole abortion healing experience, and I hate it! I hate this stupid workbook Bible study, I hate thinking about all of this, and I shouldn't have to do this stupid thing on my own!!! I want to cry, want to scream, I want to curse like a freakin' sailor! I just get so angry when I think of all this crap, when I think of what I have to do and face to "heal" from my abortion. It is so much easier to avoid and deny. Why am I even doing this?! It seems so pointless right now . . . this whole thing sucks.

Ann is so patient. She listens and just allows me to experience all the stages of grief. And after all the talking and all the processing and all the feelings, eventually, finally, *freedom.* Slowly the detached parts of myself begin to come back together. I had separated myself from my body and my emotions the way I separate myself from sex. But body and soul, womb and spirit, it's all bound up together. And we can't be whole if we have divided ourselves.

I know I have a long way to go, but right now, I'm experiencing another level of freedom. The lies and the hiding and the secrets are being stripped away and I know I'm getting closer to being who I was created to be: unhindered and free before God and others.

I faced the pain and I walked through it, and it didn't kill me.

I *can* face my pain, and every time I do, every time I trust God to walk it through and let it have its process, I'm becoming more and more free.

God has used all this pain to help me see that something is wrong. When I'm in pain, there is a reason; I just have to be brave enough and curious enough to pursue it as God brings it up. And with Him, I can have the courage to face it, feel it, and let Him do His healing work. Which I keep learning that He does, so tenderly.

The more healing that God invites me into, the more I find my heart getting softer; my walls of protection coming down. It's an exhale, this ability to feel with clarity, knowing *why* I'm hurting instead of just hurting, and letting what's true be true.

Having an abortion hurt me; it hurt me in the deep places of my soul, places I thought I could cover up and just go on. My baby is fine, safe with Jesus, but I was not fine. Healing from my abortion has freed me up in so many ways.

I have also learned through this abortion healing process that being sexually violated emotionally and physically has also hurt me in deep places of my soul, and I have hurt people by acting out of these wounds. Sin and pain and how we act out of it is complicated.

But the more I'm willing to face it and deal with it and believe the truth and face reality and throw off what is hindering me, the healthier I will be and the less damage I will do to myself and others.

Thank God I don't have to go it alone.

> He heals the brokenhearted
> and binds up their wounds. (Ps. 147:3)

CHAPTER 16

The Accusation

My six-month commitment away from my mom is over, and I decide to go visit her. *God keeps calling me to stay in relationship with her.*

I don't know why it comes up, but mom tells me she had an abortion. She says this in passing, like it's no big deal, and yet she is communicating by the vacant stare in her eyes that it actually is a big deal; I can see it hurts her. She says she doesn't want to talk about it.

She looks past me and, even though she doesn't want to talk about it, she keeps talking about it. She says she had the abortion after me and before my sister. She tells me that she always wanted a son and she thinks maybe that was her chance at one.

I just listen.

Later when I read her journals, I learn that she had an abortion when she was a teenager as well. I find the receipt for it all these years later among her things.

I have questions for Mom, about what happened when my sister and I were young, about the accusations. I know I have to step carefully with this topic. Aside from its sensitive nature, there's the fact that Mom is still angry over my six-month withdrawal from her. She likes to bring it up from time to time, about how much it hurt her. I have given up trying to explain the why, because she just won't hear it. My time would be better spent banging my head on a wall than on trying to get her to see where I'm coming from. Instead of engaging her jabs, I've learned to first, mostly ignore them, second, employ the boundary technique Bald Man taught me, and third, remember that I have released her from any motherly expectations. I see her now as a woman who is difficult, but who I can love without expectation. The only reason I haven't walked away is because I know I'm called to keep loving her. It's the whole *love your enemies* thing I guess. I try to remember that she is made in the image of God and is worthy of love. I still pray my impossible prayer that she will stop drinking, but I have no hope of it. Instead, I accept her the way she is right now. Well, as best I can. I'm only human.

I take a deep breath. I need to ask her.

I know I'm walking across a field of land mines, but I need to know our history and understand it.

"Mom, please tell me about the abuse allegations the summer I couldn't see you. I want to know what happened."

Her fingers are in her hair, looping strands and pulling on them with quick movements. Her knee is bouncing. She inhales on her cigarette, *1 . . . 2 . . . 3 . . . exhale.*

She takes a drink and while I wait to see if she's going to talk to me about it, my mind slides back to the summer of 1989. I'm nine years old . . .

My dad comes into my room and kneels near my bed. He tells me that I won't be able to see my mom this summer. I don't understand.

A few days (weeks?) later, my small hand is held firmly in my dad's hand as we enter a building I don't recognize. I think my dad said I was here to talk to someone, but my mind flits around and I don't remember. He lets go of my hand once we walk into the room with the long brown table. I see a woman with yellow-white hair, short, and she smiles at us. The tummy tightening is starting. *Why are we here?* Dad tells me to stay with this woman so she can talk to me. I don't want to stay; I want to be with my dad. He tells me all I have to do is call for him and he'll come right in. Okay. I let him go.

Two cloth dolls are on the table. I sit in front of them and the woman sits opposite me. She starts asking me questions about my mom and if my mom has ever hurt me or locked me out in the rain. *What? No.* She asks me to pick up the dolls and name them. I named the one doll Susan, my mom's name, which I immediately regret because it seems she will use that information against my mom. She tells me to have one doll undress the other doll. I don't want to do it. She prompts me again, this time telling me to have "Susan" take the clothes off the other doll. My fingertips touch the cloth doll. There's a pulsing in my neck I can feel in my ears. I start to do what she tells me but before I can, my voice is screaming for my dad and he doesn't hesitate—he's in that room in a second and I'm in his safe arms getting his shirt wet. "I want to leave!"

We walk out and never go back. My dad is my hero.

———

Mom puts her glass down, and except for the ice cubes, it's empty. She's ready, she's going to talk.

"When Keitha was four I was accused of molesting her. It's sick, telling me I would do that to my daughter! She was with her dad when the accusations came about." Mom's hands are shaking. She takes another drag. Her voice has an edge to it. "I passed two lie detector tests. I wasn't allowed to see you or Keitha. She had to have been brainwashed. They brought up how we would sleep in the same bed and scratch each other's arms, they twisted it to say I was doing gross things with my own kids! It's perverted! It was eventually dismissed. I don't want to talk about it anymore, okay?"

"Okay."

She gets up, goes inside, and makes another drink.

———

My sister doesn't remember much, but she does remember people coaching her, telling her what to say about my mom.

Later I talk to Mom's fourth husband, Military Man, and he fills in the gaps. Here's what he tells me:

> The first I heard of it was when your mom called me on the phone when I was at work. She said, "They have come and taken Keitha!"
>
> I listen on the phone as your mom tells me her daughter is gone, that Keitha's dad's family came with the sheriff and took her. We find out they took her because Susan had been accused of molesting Keitha. I told her we could get married and pull our resources together to fight this and get Keitha back. She had no other support, not from her dad or her brothers. She felt like she had been left on an island by herself. Keitha was gone about a year. No one would tell us where she was. We hired a private investigator and finally found her in Flagstaff, Arizona. We flew out with a court order and brought Keitha back. DCFS (Division of Children and Family Services) intervened but no charges were brought forth.

Mom's Journal | September 27, 1989 | Mom's note to her lawyer

This is my position:

> I strongly deny having sexually
>   molested my daughter.
> I strongly desire custody of my child.

Mom's letter to me when I'm nine | July 18, 1989 | The summer I can't see my mom

Hello Sarah,

How are you, honey? I wish I could be there with you right now and see you for myself. I've been wishing for that a lot lately. I miss you so very, very much, Sarah. Thoughts of you never fail to brighten up my day. As a matter of fact, I can't think of anything that has made me smile more these days than talking to you on the telephone! You are such a joy to talk to. You are so smart and funny too. I feel so proud to have had a magnificent daughter as wonderful as you are. Every day I think of you and silently send to Pennsylvania all the love in my heart and pray you feel it. It's been real hard for both of us, I know, to understand what is happening right now. I think it is one of the most wrong situations I have ever seen, and I don't like it one bit. I've tried and tried and tried to get the Children's Services case workers to look for the truth in what I say, but they are not listening. They are so wrapped up in keeping us apart, and thinking it is right, when they should also be asking themselves the "million-dollar question": could they be wrong?—answer?: You bet they could and they are! Why can't they see things straight? Why are they so blind? What is the major problem in believing us? Oh Sarah, I'm so sorry for the way things have turned out this summer. It's really not my fault, nor yours, and I'm even more sorry that you and I have to suffer such sadness for reasons we don't understand. Keep your spirits up and don't lose faith (even for one second!) that everything will be alright soon, and we'll be able to visit with each other, in person, to make up for lost time. Meanwhile, honey, I want you to never, never, ever forget that I love you immensely, and I always will no matter what. You are my sunshine on a cloudy day. I thank God for bringing you into this world; I'll not ever stop being thankful. XXXOOOOXXOOXX Mom <3

CHAPTER 17

Search Me, God

Pain keeps showing up and inviting me to pay attention.

Talking to my mom about the past, about Keitha and the gutting accusations, is helping me to understand my mom a little better. Her wound is still open and when I ask to know more, she bleeds in order to tell me. Between the unfulfilled desire to be unconditionally loved by her father (she tells me that's what she's always wanted) and the year of fighting for her dignity and her children after the accusations, I can see how one drink led to another. I think about her pain, the pain of all of it and how unbearable it must have been and how feeling the pain was just too much. *I can relate.*

I escaped my pain by using my body and she escaped her pain with alcohol.

I wonder if my mom had had support and love if maybe she would have been able to sit in the pain and listen to its truth and grieve for what was lost? What if she knew she didn't have to carry the pain and grief on her own, or that when she thought God wasn't near, He was actually sitting *with* her, grieving with her? What if she knew, "The God and Father of our Lord Jesus Christ, the Father of mercies and God of all comfort, who comforts us in all our affliction . . ." (2 Cor. 1:3–4)?

Maybe she did know. Maybe she knew He loved her despite the drinking and the neglect and the cruelty she bestowed to her daughters. Maybe He saw what I couldn't see, *what I can't see*—all the ways her brokenness led her to breaking others.

Maybe this is how God sees every one of us and it's why He has compassion for the world, why He died for the world and desires everyone to be saved from the slavery of sin and the wreckage it produces.

I don't know, but I know that I want to keep loving my mom, even though it's hard and it hurts. I want God to search me and get rid of everything that is getting in the way of me being able to love.

> Search me, O God, and know my heart!
> Try me and know my thoughts!
> And see if there be any grievous way
>   in me,
> and lead me in the way everlasting!
> (Ps. 139:23–24)

Search Me, O God, and Know My Heart

At night, in bed, I whisper this prayer: *"Search me, O God."*

What I'm asking when I say, "search me," is really this: "What's in my heart, God, that I'm not seeing? Where is this problem coming from, what is the root, and what do You want me to know? I'm wide open to You, Lord, so show me if there's something You want me to see."

So often I try to cover the nakedness of my heart, pretending (or honestly thinking) I'm fine. Just like Adam and Eve in the garden tried to hide their nakedness, I sometimes think that if God were to *see* me, He would be disappointed in me or find me out for who I really am. The truth is, just as God knew exactly where Adam and Eve were in the garden when he called to them, He already knows who I am and all the places in my heart I think are hidden.

And as for searching my own heart, well, I only know so much. Plus, it makes me neurotic. God already knows every piece of my heart, every crevice and crack, and He is the only one who knows how to rightly navigate it. Without God, without being let in to what He knows and sees, I only get a partial picture of my brokenness and my sin. I want Him to search the deep places of my heart and as He sees fit, begin the work necessary to set me free where there is bondage.

Try Me and Know My Anxious Thoughts

Here I am, God. You've searched me out; now examine me, test me, *prove what's in me and what I'm made of.*

I pray those words with trepidation. Do I really want God to test me? *What is it I am anxious about, Lord? I have You, and You give me a peace that surpasses all understanding (Phil. 4:7), so what is happening with these thoughts that keep me up at night?*

It's a profound peace knowing that God knows my anxious thoughts and what they're made of. He will show me what is fallen brain chemistry and/or what is circumstantial, and how they may overlap. I know His gentle examination of me will reveal what I need to know in order to gain more freedom.

See My Offensive Ways

I know I am complicated, but I'm also daily contending with my sin. I know I'm righteous before God and perfect according to heaven because of Jesus, but on this side of eternity, I still have offensive ways.

When I ask God to see my offensive ways, it's not that He can't see them already, it's that I'm *inviting* Him in to show *me* what they are so that, with His help, I can turn from them in humility and grow instead in love, joy, peace, patience, kindness, goodness, faithfulness, gentleness, and self-control (Gal. 5:22–23). I don't want to be in bondage to any sin, so I'm willing to face my offensive ways in order to be free.

Lead Me in the Everlasting Way

I love this phrase. I want to be led into the way that matters, the forever way, the way that sheds all the things that don't matter, that hinder me, that keep me from loving God and others.

As God searches me and sees me and examines me, as He gently reveals the offensive ways in order that I may repent, He then leads me into the way that leads to life.

And the life He offers is not one of escape, but one of wholeness and goodness and victory.

Mom's Journal | April 30, 2006 | At this writing, I'm married and have a child and mom and I are still in relationship, though we rarely see each other in person. Mom is still grappling with feeling alone and unloved by her family, especially with her dad. I have no idea how lonely she really is.

I am beginning to recognize the fact that in order to survive and help others I have to accept the fact that I'm not unconditionally loved (except for my girls) . . . something I strongly desired all my life, but there have been enough real-life stories to prove that hasn't been the case. I have to embrace that in order to get over myself and move on, I must try to put myself in second or third place, but not first . . . I am over a half century old, if I am to do good works I need to get started on trying for that instead of clinging onto the stuff that sets me back.

I smoked pot after many, many years of leaving it behind . . . I have left it behind again, and do not even miss it . . . that's the Jesus part . . . don't even miss it! I truly believe that the same can hold true for the alcohol fix I have fixated on. Cigarettes too. It's not that I have an aversion to these things, but I think I have had enough of them, don't want to be dependent on them, because I have realized what a pain it is to have to go to the store to acquire them (oh, so distressing and energy-consuming). I have not liked HAVING to have them . . . like I have believed all my life that I am not worth [expletive] if the family I grew up with doesn't think I am worth a [expletive]. I figure I will stop closer to freedom. If I give up (since Mom died) the idea of my dad and brothers giving a [expletive] about whether I am dead or alive or worthy of respect from them (heck, I am not even sure if Mom liked me), perhaps I can give up the self-destructive behavior that I bring upon myself in the name of love . . . sounds crazy, but true. Could work, at least it's a new approach I should try. I am considering it, and with the help of Jesus I know it is possible, because it is because of Him I am still holding onto me . . . I do not know what that's worth, but He seems to . . . I would like to play out that scenario. Now I am going to get even more personal.

My wishes for the future:

- To be a great positive influence on my grandchildren and my two wonderful children.

- To feel a sense of pride (instead of dread at the mention of my name or behavior).

- Make a decent living independently of relying on others to get me by (financially).

- Doing something for other people by sharing something only I knew for brief periods of time in my life, the sort of stuff that would inspire them to persevere, embrace nature and all the wonderful things that encompass it . . . to live and not let the light of their passion fade.

Sounds romantic; I hope I have something to give.

CHAPTER 18

Jesse

The first thing I notice is his legs. They're nice. I know, it's absurd.

His name is Jesse and he's my college mentor/ friend's younger brother. Way younger, *too much younger*; I shouldn't be looking at him. He's a baby, a freshman, and I'm a junior. In college years, that's a huge gap. I'm heading into my senior year and then out into the great big world to find a job, and he'll still be in class, closer to high school than college graduation. But he has these intense blue eyes that I can't get out of my mind.

He's also kind and sweet and gentle.

Fast-forward to fall of my senior year and Jesse tells me how much he likes me. *Go on.* I tell him he's sweet, and I like him too, but we need to take it slow because I'm the relationship girl, the girl who goes from guy to guy and I don't want to be that girl. I've barely been single a minute and Lord knows I need to learn to be content without a guy. He says he understands, but then he adds, "I want to pursue you for marriage." *Oh, Jesse.*

We date for six months, and by "date" I mean we have two-hour conversations each night because he's at a campus three hours away. I have learned that being alone in an apartment isn't wise for me, so I invite my dear friend Lois to be my roommate. We are a kindred match, both possessing the ability to completely ignore a messy apartment. She is a faithful friend and she prays for me and encourages me, and we eat Pringles together while sitting on the kitchen floor crying and laughing and staying up way too late.

She ends up being a bridesmaid in my wedding.

After only six months of "taking it slow," Jesse asks me to marry him. Four months later we're husband and wife. And I'll tell you what sealed the deal for me.

I wanted my mom to meet Jesse and I wanted Jesse to meet my mom. She's a part of my life for better or for worse, so he should know what he's getting into. We drive fourteen hours to Bowdon, Georgia, and we pull up to that familiar house with that smoky screened-in porch. *Here we go.*

The first couple of days are good—all is well. But as usual, Mom and I can't leave well enough alone. She starts in on me. I know how to deal with this; it's okay. It sucks, and I have to take some deep breaths in order to maintain, but I'm good. I'm mostly good. *Crap, I'm not good.* And apparently, neither is Jesse. He stands up and tells my mom in the most respectful way possible that she will not talk to me like that anymore. *Whaaa?* I'm dumbfounded. Is he . . . *defending me*? My mom is dumbfounded. We're basically frozen and Jesse looks at me, takes my hand, and after packing up quickly, we leave.

He enforced a boundary and doesn't even know the bald man with the leather jacket. He's just emotionally healthy and apparently a member of the knighthood.

It's a wonder I didn't marry him that night.

Mom came to town for our wedding. She wore a beautiful butter-colored dress and had her hair professionally styled, pulled up at the sides with long blonde ringlets falling down past her shoulders. She looked lovely.

———

Our first year of marriage was awful. I mean, truth be told, we were about ready to divorce as we pulled up to our hotel in Marco Island for our honeymoon. I don't think he knew what he was getting into with me. I didn't know how to be in a marriage, how to act, how to not run or be a jerk or name-call. I knew sarcasm and manipulation. I knew how to cut. I was so wretched that on our one-year anniversary I put on my wedding dress (which I could no longer zip up), cooked dinner, and when he walked in from work said, "Surprise!"

He looked me and started crying. He sat on the floor of our apartment and he cried and said, "You actually love me."

Yeah, I do.

Mom's Journal | February 27, 2003 | This is the year I marry Jesse. Mom's constant source of heartbreak is that she feels unloved by her family.

My entry today is some awful stuff, but the stuff of which is in my mind. I'm sick and tired of my family relationships as I've seen them up close the last two months. My immediate family's opinion of me is biased on the negative, always has been. I've come to the realization that it will never change, no matter what I do or say. Quite frankly, the family acceptance and love I've yearned for as long as I can remember will not be forthcoming. I believe these days, it will never happen. I am now convinced that no matter what I may do for good, I'm only remembered within this family as a burden, a convenient scapegoat for whatever ills them, and a source of ridicule, an easy target, so to speak, because I allow it. Hate to say this, but I don't want to live in this world anymore, simply begging for unconditional love, which, to me should be natural within a family, and not receiving it since the day I was born, and I'll be fifty this year. As much as I hate it, these days, it doesn't matter to me at this point, that's the bottom line. If the folks who are supposed to love you because they are your family don't respond to the good in you, and only relate to you in negative terms, what's the point? Drag down, guilt, disappointment, hurt, pain, emotional stuff . . . I don't see how I can move away from the negative if I'm choosing to be enmeshed in it. I no longer desire to hold onto the hope that peace and love will exist between myself and my blood relatives, notably my brothers and dad.

Good news is, I'm convinced that perhaps Mother and I connected for a brief time these last two months with my dedication to being there with her while she's sick. I tell myself all that matters is the hardship I put on my family by trying to hold onto the only home I've known. I tell myself to let go, relieve them of their hardship and relieve myself of trying to hold onto it on a purely financial basis. I'm sick of it, and praise God, I have enough faith that He will lead me.

What have I got to lose if I don't give in to them? Well, there's my soft, comfortable bed, security I've found in my home—safety I'd not known before, but I hate to have to come to the conclusion that the price I pay emotionally is a good trade-off. I lose everything I have, and they just gain more.

Dear Lord, if I am wrong, please let me know in Your gentle way. If I am right, please give me the strength of conviction to make it so.

I love You, Susan

CHAPTER 19

Poppy

It's a year after our wedding and Jesse and I decide to go visit Mom.

She has moved into a small, dark trailer in the backwoods of Bowdon that she shares with her little Jack Russell Terrier named Beans. Buddy died years ago.

My mom's dad, Poppy, tells her she has to leave her house, the one I lived in when I lived with her, because she's not making the payments on it. Or maybe it's because he wants to give the house to his son. I don't know, but I know he owns it and she doesn't have a choice.

So she moves into a trailer (Poppy owns this too) and her brother and his wife move into the other house, our house.

I always liked my Poppy. I spent so many days at his house, with Grandma, swimming in their pool, enjoying tuna sandwiches, playing dress-up in the attic, and being tucked into clean, Downy-smelling sheets when I'd spend the night. As I got older though, I saw how Poppy treated Mom, always telling her (with a smile on his face and patronizing laugh) how dumb she was. He said this to her and he said it *to me* about her. I can't recall a single visit to his house—a few miles from where Mom lived—when he did not insult her in some way. She was good at hiding how much his words hurt her, so good that I didn't know the pain she felt until years later. She always responded to his insults with, "Oh, Dad."

Jesse and I sit down in the small living room and wait while Mom makes a drink. I look over at her, and the scar on her forehead, the dent, reminds me about the time Mom said Poppy kicked her into the edge of a table.

I asked Mom once how she got such an extensive vocabulary, always using words I had to learn the definitions to. She told me that Poppy would drill words into her, and when she would get them wrong, he'd hit her.

When I lived with Mom, there were times when we'd be driving somewhere, and a memory would come to her about Poppy and she would just start talking about it. "When I was sixteen years old I came out of the shower and had a towel around me. Dad pushed me into my room and onto my bed and lied down on top of me. He told me if I didn't want to be treated like a tramp I shouldn't dress like one."

Mom has never felt accepted by her family. She knows she's a disappointment to them; her dad reminds her of this all the time. He nags her about her drinking and smoking and money habits. He sees her as a leech. He laughs at her, berates her. But she loves him—he's her father—and so she keeps going back to him and he keeps treating her like dirt. What self-confidence she does have is held up by God alone. Her deepest desire is for him to love her unconditionally, although she's resigned to the fact that it won't happen.

Mom sits down and we all catch up and shoot the breeze. I feel safe and confident having Jesse with me. Mom likes Jesse.

When Mom gets under my skin, I walk away, I ask God to help me, and I forgive her. Over and over and over I forgive her. The mother-wound isn't gone, but it's not nearly as tender as it once was. I choose to keep loving her because I know that God loves her, and I love Him, and He tells me to love her. When the wound bleeds, I take it to Him, and with Him I cry out all my frustrations and hurt places. And then I pray again and again for her to know His love and to stop drinking.

Not long after our visit, Mom gets out of that musty trailer when a friend from Florida visits and insists she move down to New Port Richey with her. She'll help her get a place, a nice trailer in a 50+ community. *God's face is shining upon her.*

She moves to Florida.

And then, the impossible happens.

Email to Mom from Poppy | Date Unknown

It is very lonely without your mother. Sure wish I had a stable, sober daughter to turn to in these times. Maybe someday God will give my daughter back to me.

Love, Dad

Mom's Journal | Date Unknown

If the torture would be done, life could begin, and a greater peace would be mine. I could be me! Sure, I know being me doesn't mean that I have to have a homestead, but this is the least he owes me. I could settle my losses, accept the lack of family love, the disrespect, being disregarded, unacknowledged, ignored, the disgust of me for no good reason, the wasted time I spent buying into their illusions making them so (because I believed them) and their lies. The values, importance, and benefits of living and believing in yourself was taken from me. Simply because I was me and not who they wanted me to be. You [Dad] owe me a life of my own; give me a starting line and get away from me, because you well know I can't get away from you. Stop the madness, there'd be no skin off your rear-end to make it so. Do it. Set me free from my hated belief that you don't and never have cared, that your only daughter was/is worth abusing. Allow me to believe I was worth being born because y'all have always had homes and places to spare. *I just need one.* I can't stand the thought of my children worrying about their mother homeless. Surely you can conceive that? I cannot allow you to hurt them by denying me my due. I earned it; you owe me. But number one, you cannot cause pain to my girls because you abhor me. Don't, as you have the choice not to. Don't. Please. But I know you will, but, I don't want to know that; I don't like believing it because it makes me sick.

Help Me Be Me, Set Me Free

CHAPTER 20

The Impossible

"Hello?" I answer the phone breathlessly after dragging my sick behind off the couch.

It's September '08 and I'm three months along with my third baby, sick as a dog with morning sickness. And when I say morning I mean *all day.*

"Yes, this is she," I reply.

"I wanted to call you and let you know that your mom is in the hospital here in Port Richey. She has stage 4 cirrhosis of the liver, the end stage, and she's not going to live long. If you are able, you should make plans to visit her as soon as possible."

"What? Okay . . . uh . . ."

I ask the woman if I can talk to my mom. She says I can, and she puts me through to her room.

"Mom, what happened? How did you end up in the hospital? How are you feeling?"

"Well, I'm here because God told me to stop drinking."

"WHAT?"

She tells me the story of "the voice."

"I got up and, like I do every morning, made my drink of Vodka and 7Up. I went and sat on down on my couch and was about to take my first sip when I heard the voice. The voice commanded me to put my drink down. 'You do not need it, do not want it, you do not even like the taste of it.' It was so powerful and so true that I knew that God was the one leading me, and *I listened*. Without taking a sip I rose from the couch, headed to the kitchen sink, and poured it down the drain."

She goes on to tell me how she went through days of withdrawal that nearly killed her. She would wake up and "see" rain in her hallway. She would look out the bedroom window and "see" people laughing at her. After a few days of blacking out, hallucinations, and physical pain, she finally called a friend and got to the hospital. The doctor couldn't believe she had survived withdrawal on her own.

My mouth is literally hanging open. Words are stuck wherever it is that words get stuck and I am just stunned silent. "Hello?" Mom asks into the phone.

"I'm here. I'm on my way."

I get to Florida, and when I see my mom, I see eyes that are the color of vanilla pudding and skin that looks like it's been soaked in a bath of yellow dye. And what is up with her belly? She looks eight months pregnant. She says it's the ascites, a common by-product of cirrhosis, that causes her belly to be so huge. She has to get it drained weekly.

"The doctor says I have a month to live, maybe two."

"I know," I reply.

I still can't believe she quit drinking. I just can't believe it's real. It is.

We spend the week in her home going through her bills and trying to get her affairs in order. It's overwhelming. When we tire of the paperwork, we go sit at the pool. The water and the sun ease my sickness.

There are no final moving words, no revelations, no tied-up-with-a-bow phrases that ease the heartache of the past. No, those things aren't here, but God is here, and He is kind and He put the fire that used to rage in me out a long time ago.

I hug Mom goodbye and promise to call.

Mom's Journal | October 23, 2008 | After Mom quits drinking

Praise the Lord!

I've got to say that no vodka is very, very special and a huge blessing to my quality of life. That's where it all started, my new life and ways of living. God is transforming me into the being He created me to be, only this time, I am "armed" with experience and lessons only life can reveal. Before it's all over, He will show me the path I was created to tread. He is with me, I feel it, and I not only feel it, I know it! It's so exciting. I feel like a child, mouth agape, seeing this world for the very first time.

Praise the Lord!

CHAPTER 21

Mom Moves In

Mom doesn't die.

Several months roll by and now I have a new baby girl. Mom comes to visit. She meets her grandkids for the first time. She holds them, and they squeeze her and kiss her, and she is *glowing*. But she looks bad, and when I take her back to the airport, I'm worried about her. I wish she didn't live so far away.

Jesse and I move into a new house, right next door to his parents' house where he grew up. It's a sweet little semi-detached home, and it has something I am just so tickled about: a playroom for the kids. Downstairs is a huge room, one that I envision turning from playroom to homeschool room. I dream up what our days will look like spent in that room and make plans to decorate it, filling it with our books and puzzles and toys.

But as I'm dreaming, a thought intrudes, gently, but persistently: *Mom could live in this room. We could take her in and take care of her and she wouldn't have to die alone.*

No. No, no, nope, that is crazy.

She's sick. She's dying.

She's difficult and stubborn and I can only tolerate being around her for short stretches of time—like, a few days. Live with us?

She's always wanted to be a part of a family. She's never had one, not really. It will not be easy, but you will not be alone.

Crap.

That night in bed I tell Jesse that I think my mom should move in with us. "I don't want her to die alone." Jesse is understandably hesitant.

"Do you know what you're asking? Do you really?"

"Yes."

We make the decision that we will invite her to live with us.

She says yes, and within the month, Poppy drives her to Pennsylvania and she moves in. The playroom is now her room, and she has her bed and her furniture and her TV. She loves watching *Doctor Who*.

We have in-home hospice care for her, and Tina, her nurse, is perfect for Mom. She's calm and kind and patient.

Jesse sits down with Tina and Mom as Mom fills out paperwork from hospice. One of the questions on the form says, "Is there anything you want people to know before you die?"

Mom writes, "I want my daughters to know that I love them very much."

Within a month of Mom moving in with us, Jesse finds a bad sore on his back and goes to the doctor. The doctor looks at Jesse and says, "Well, it looks like you have shingles."

"I thought only old people got shingles?"

"Well, generally, yes. It's usually found in younger people when they're under a lot of stress. Are you under any stress?"

After a pause Jesse replies, "My mother-in-law is living with us."

Doc responds, "That's probably it!"

———

Living with Mom is like living with a child.

She's as stubborn and as frustrating as ever. She is always complaining about the kids running around upstairs, their feet pounding on the floor above her room. They are toddlers. She likes to correct my parenting, which would be funny if it weren't so aggravating, and whenever Jesse and I argue, she's right there to say, "I agree with Jesse." Every time. Jesse responds with, "You're not helping, Suzy." Mom mumbles and walks back to her room. Speaking of her room, she has brought Florida to it, keeping it at 85–90 degrees all the time.

"Suzy, I'm going to the grocery store, need anything?" Jesse asks Mom every time he goes out.

"Nope." As soon as we get back she needs fifteen things.

"Why didn't you tell us?"

"I didn't remember."

Mom sits on our front stoop to smoke.

On a particularly snowy day, our neighbor Brandy brings her dog out to go to the bathroom. We share a yard, so some of the yellow is on our side, near the stoop. Mom can't help herself and she says, "You shouldn't let your dog go to the bathroom in our yard. It's disgusting."

In between inhales she makes passive-aggressive comments. Brandy goes back inside. We like Brandy. We have a good relationship with Brandy. She's a wonderful neighbor. Mom is messing with this.

Mom starts sitting on Brandy's stoop, on her little white bench, and smokes right there by Brandy's front door. "I just love this bench. You don't mind if I smoke here, do you." It's not a question; it's more of a statement. Brandy is at a loss for words. Jesse explains to Brandy that Mom is sick, and we're so sorry.

But it's not all bad. Some of it is a gift.

We always get a kick out of it when she comes upstairs, says something funny, starts laughing at herself, and then goes back down. She's so silly. And when she comes up, she always has her fluffy socks on, and they are never pulled up right, so there is always fluff at the end of her foot. She's kind of cute in a ridiculous way.

She takes the kids and me out to breakfast each week with her small amount of Social Security money. She loves breakfast and always orders eggs Benedict. At dinner, and this has happened more than once, we'll be eating and one of her rotting teeth will fall out into her food. "Oops." She laughs uproariously with food still in her mouth.

But the real gift is the times we spend together that seem carved out for us by God. These times aren't spent in deep, meaningful conversation, but we're together, not fighting, getting a second chance with each other. We laugh together. We share meals together. We love each other in the ways that we are able. It's wildly imperfect and there are plenty of frustrations and prayers offered up when living together feels unbearable. But we push through, in grace, believing there is something sacred even in this hard love.

Nine Lives

One day I walk upstairs, and Mom is standing in the living room, staring at nothing.

She has a glass of water in her hand. Her hand is shaking.

"Mom?"

She pours the glass of water out onto the floor. I rush over to her and take the glass and set it down. She pulls her pants down. She's confused, and she's not responding to me. I call Tina and tell her what's happening. She tells me she's on her way.

I get my mom to sit down. I sit with her, and I wait for Tina. Now I'm shaking.

Tina arrives, and I ask her what's happening. I hear the panic in my voice, but I manage to push down the tears.

"It might be time for her to go to the in-patient hospice." In-patient hospice is where you go to die.

"Tina, I'm not ready."

"It's going to be okay," she says gently.

We get to the hospice facility and they put her into a bed and give her all kinds of medicine. She's quiet, sleeping. I talk with the doctor and she says that Mom could likely pass away within a few days. I spend each day with her, and I bring the kids with me and they watch movies or color or run around as I chase them. I'm there for several hours each night while Jesse watches the kids at home. I don't feel scared or sad or much of anything really. It's odd. I guess there's a part of my heart that is just closed up. Maybe mourning the loss of my mom has made her real death easier. I don't know.

One morning while at the hospice I go get some coffee from the common room, and when I come back to Mom's room, she's not in the bed. I look around, check the bathroom, and am baffled. Glancing up toward the windows, I see the outside door, the one that goes directly outside, is cracked open. *Is that smoke?* Just outside the door is Mom, sitting on a chair, smoking a cigarette.

This woman has nine lives.

She is released from in-patient hospice, something that rarely happens.

We go see a liver specialist and the doctor is telling us all about how her small liver is, *blah blah blah,* medical jargon, and then says to my mom with us there, "We can't tell you how long you have to live, but you're okay for now, just keep taking your medicine."

Jesse perks up and says to the doctor, "So wait a minute, she's going to be okay?"

"Yes, as long as she takes her medicine."

Jesse tells me later that his next hidden thought was, *Well, time to start looking for a place!*

After a year and a half of living with us, out-patient hospice releases my mom as well. We say goodbye to Tina and thank her for all her help and kindness.

We tell Mom it's time to move out. "We'll help you find a place. You could live near us, and I could be around if anything happens to you or you need help."

Mom insists on moving to Florida where it's warm and where she can swim. We don't stand in her way.

Mom's Journal | April 2010 | Written while Mom lived with us

Yesterday I told Sarah I was feeling a hankering for human contact (which hasn't happened since I arrived here almost three months ago). I had asked her to put aside the computer for fifteen minutes a day for us to do some coffee-talking. I made plans to have our coffee tomorrow while catching some sun. She broke "the plan" as if it were nothing, blaming Caroline's schedule. So here I am, the "martyr." There is always an excuse why she can't talk with me for fifteen minutes a day . . . I get the feeling she does not want that fifteen minutes a day, and that is kinda odd, don't you think?

CHAPTER 22

Sorry

It's been several years since I've seen Mom.

We talk on the phone from time to time and all that hanging up I had to do in the past is long gone.

When I do talk to her, she seems happy. She swims every day in the apartment pool, goes to a Bible study, and has made some good friends. *I never know how lonely she really is.* Jesse says I should go visit her in Florida, where she's now living in a low-income senior apartment. We don't know how long she has to live (although I'm convinced she has nine lives) so I make a plan to visit her in May, just for a few days.

After getting lost a few times, I drive my rental car into the parking lot of her building. *This is low-income housing?* At the entrance is a portico, with four huge, crisp, white columns. The siding is a fresh light yellow, and all up and down the building are white railings, porches for each apartment. I walk into the lobby and it's gorgeous, with tile floors, two small couches facing each other, and flowers on accent tables. To my right is a salon. I keep walking forward into another, the common room (which I later learn is called the clubhouse), and it is filled with nice furniture. There's a fireplace surrounded by stone and a flat-screen TV on the wall. Windows are as tall as doors, bright light filling the space. Outside I can see a large pond with a walking path around it. I walk back into the lobby and wait for Mom; she's on her way down to get me.

My breath catches. I'm not ready for what I see.

Her lips are squished up and thin, making her chin pronounced. Her eyes are big, but that's because her face is so small, pulled in behind her cheekbones. She's thin, but she still has her ascites belly, although it isn't as bad as it used to be. Her hair is long, colored blonde, with gray peeking through. Her nose is sharper than it used to be.

She has a gold cross hanging on her neck, just above the neckline of her shin-length tan cotton dress.

I smile big and go to her. I hug her, and she timidly hugs me back. She tells me she's sorry about her face but she didn't feel like putting her upper dentures in, that's why her lips are all squished up. "You got dentures!"

"Yes, they were so cheap here, Poppy even paid for them!"

"How's it going with you and Poppy?"

"Oh, you know, same old, same old Dad."

I'm still stunned at how nice this place is, and I'm so happy for her that she gets to live here. She takes me up to her apartment and as soon as we walk in, it's familiar. It looks like Mom. There are things everywhere, papers and pictures and knickknacks. But she straightened up for me, and I can tell she takes pride in her home.

She puts in her top dentures for me, and the false teeth bring structure to her face. She's still pretty, even though the years and alcohol and the smoking have made their mark. She's been sober nine years now. I shake my head just thinking about the miracle of it.

The next day she wants to introduce me to her friends. Every morning in the clubhouse there are donuts and coffee and residents hanging out with each other, talking and laughing and complaining about all that needs done to the building. We walk to a table with about four or five people and she introduces me. She tells them I'm her wonderful first-born and that I'm an author. *She's proud of me.*

We put on our bathing suits and go to the pool. It's an oblong pool surrounded by lounge chairs and palm trees. The weather is perfection at around 80 degrees. The water is glorious.

Later that night while I'm stuffing my face with pizza from a local pizza place, Mom gets agitated and starts in on me. I yell, "Stop! Just stop it." I didn't mean to yell; it just came out. Before I could tell her

I was sorry, she did something I can't remember her ever doing. EVER.

She says to me, "I'm sorry. I shouldn't have done that."

I literally do not remember a time my mom has ever told me sorry in any way other than a sarcastic, *whatever, I'm sorry because you're offended* kind of way. No, she just said she was sorry. No sarcasm.

And then, as if that wasn't enough, she tells me she's sorry for not being a good mom.

"The Lord has been showing me the truth about how I treated you and how I hurt you and I'm sorry, Sarah. I want to make things right."

Am I in a dream? This isn't supposed to happen. I gave this up, this hope; I mourned it. It's dead.

I have to steady myself because even though I'm frozen for a minute, unsure if this is real, I could have fallen right out of my chair.

She's sorry. I'm not crazy. She did hurt me, and she knows it, and now she's sorry. I'm looking at her face and what she's saying is real.

I don't know how to respond. All I can manage is, "Thank you."

Oh God, thank You. Thank You for this. Thank You.

Mom's Journal | 2013 | Mom is sober and living in Florida

I've begun writing again, for Sarah, who keeps pleading with me to write. Hopefully I can "inspire her" and move her soul.

CHAPTER 23

The Last of Nine Lives

"The Lord told me this is my last year to live."

I'm on the phone with my mom and she's telling me about her bucket list and how she wants me to come and visit her in April. I'm not taking her seriously with the whole "last year to live" thing. My mom just keeps going, busted liver and all. I tell her I can't see her in April because I'm going to Thailand that month and it would be too much to come home and then go on another trip that same month. I tell her I can do May. She really, really wants me to see her in April, but she doesn't push it.

We make reservations to stay at a hotel on the beach in St. Petersburg, Florida. She gets us tickets to the Dali Museum, and tells me we are going to eat our hearts out with a seafood feast on the beach. I tell her I'm looking forward to it. I never consider it could be my last time seeing her alive. I certainly never consider that we won't even make the trip.

I spend ten days in Thailand working with an organization that helps to fight human trafficking. When I get home, I'm jet-lagged and exhausted. I sleep during the daytime for about a week until my body adjusts to being home. I don't call my dad or my mom to tell them I'm home safe. I just sleep and ignore the nagging feeling I should call.

A week and a half after being home from Thailand I stop over at my friend's house. We're outside talking when my phone rings. I don't recognize the number, but I think it's a Florida area code. I excuse myself, go sit down in my van, and answer the call.

"Hi, Sarah, it's *so and so* from North Bay Hospital. I need to know if we have your permission to resuscitate your mom."

"Wait, what? What are you talking about? I don't know what you're talking about."

"You don't know your mom is in the hospital?"

"No! When? What happened?"

"I'm so sorry. She was checked in on April fifth. She said you were in Thailand and not to bother you. But I really need to know if I have your permission to resuscitate her if her heart stops while she's here."

"I, uh, yes, yes, you have my permission, but can I get more information, please? I literally have no idea what's happening."

Everything around me goes dark. My hands are sticky and I can't keep them still.

"I'll have the doctor call you right away."

I wait. I can't breathe. *Breathe. Calm down. Just breathe.*

The phone rings again and a man is on the other end. All I hear is, "Mass in liver." "Blood clots in blood vessel system and spleen." "Liver is not cleaning out." "Can't treat." "Survival less than 5 percent if we do chest compressions." "Comfort measures." "Need to come soon."

The drive home is a blur. I call my sister and tell her Mom is in the hospital. She says she knows; she talked to Mom two days ago from the hospital and she's fine. They talked on the phone and Mom said she'd be getting out soon. My sister says she didn't call me because she figured I knew since I'm usually the first person to be called.

I'm now sitting outside with my computer, still on the phone, trying to find the soonest flight out. I get one for the next morning.

God, please don't let her die before I get there. Please let her see me.

Just as the plane touches down, my phone beeps with a voice mail. I have two messages from the hospital asking when I'll be there. I'm going as fast as I can! I still have a forty-minute drive from the airport.

The back of my neck is tight. My foot leans into the gas pedal. *Please don't let her die until she sees me.*

I run into the hospital and take the elevator up; I need to find room 321. My eyes are scanning room numbers, but I don't need to see where she is. I can hear her. She's yelling. There are no words, just a yell that is between a moan and a loud cry. I hurry into her room and her head is moving back and forth with her yelling. Her friend Marnie is there, talking quietly to her. I lean down to my mom. "Saree's here." Saree is what she called me when she felt affection toward me.

I rub her arm and her head. I try to look into her eyes but they won't stay still, they just keep moving back and forth. The yelling is rhythmic, every minute or so she groans and yells out.

She's alive, but *she's gone.*

———

I call Poppy and tell him Mom is in the hospital and it's really bad. He says he's sorry for *me.* He doesn't want anything to do with it. I tell him I don't want his money, I just wanted him to know. He's says, "Okay, well, thank you." Mom was right about him.

I hang up and throw the phone on the chair beside me. *Inhale, exhale, inhale, exhale.* I reach down and pick the phone back up. I call my mom's cousin Jeannie. They were close. Jeannie doesn't understand; she just talked to my mom a couple of days ago, just like my sister. Jeannie tells me Mom said she was fine and was getting out of here. She was talking about our trip to the beach and the Dali Museum and the seafood feast.

What happened between two days ago and now?

The doctor comes in to talk to me and he just keeps saying the words, "Comfort measures." I tell him we've been through this before. She's been in hospice care and I've been called and told she has a month to live, and then she lived! He tells me there's nothing more they can do and I should take her somewhere where she can pass away in comfort.

No, no this can't be the end because we haven't gone to the beach yet and we haven't had our seafood feast. She needs to see the Dali Museum.

"Mom, please, if you can hear me, please look at me. Please squeeze my hand or something."

Nothing but wide-open eyes going back and forth.

"Okay, Mom. Okay. It's okay."

I make the arrangements to have her taken to a nearby hospice facility. An ambulance will take her and I'll meet her there.

———

She's trying to get out of the hospice bed. She's yelling louder now and the nurses are trying to calm her down. "Where is the doctor? You said she would have pain medication and she would be comfortable."

"We can't get a hold of him, and we can't give her anything until he calls us back."

Half an hour goes by and the doctor still hasn't called. I'm beside myself. I call Jesse and I ask him what to do. He asks me if we can move her to another facility. I tell the nurses that I'm going to move her to another facility because this is awful. This is not what is supposed to be happening.

Just as I start to call another facility the doctor calls and the nurses are now allowed to give my mom something to calm her down. Whatever they give her works quickly. She's quiet.

I pull out the couch bed and lay my weary bones down. *Am I killing her? Should I have tried harder at the hospital to get them to do something? She was okay a few days ago.* God, this is excruciating.

Throughout the night she yells, and I hear the nurses come in and give her the quieting medicine. I listen to her breathing. My eyes hurt from crying.

The next day the doctor comes in and pulls a chair up to the end of her bed, by her feet. I ask him how long it will take for her to die. He tells me that without food and water the body could take five to seven days to shut down.

I leave tomorrow, and she will die alone, starving to death.

Mom | March 25, 2016 | Email to her cousin Jeannie written a month before her death

Hello Jeannie, nice talking to you again. I am a little kooky lately because I've had a lot on my mind. I do believe the Lord is calling me to join Him soon and so I have made a bucket list of a couple of things I'd like to do this year. Garn and Mark have pulled together some money for a trip to an art museum in St. Petersburg, Florida. I've always wanted to see it but couldn't get a ride or afford to go. Sarah is coming down here the first week of May and she's going to go with me. We got enough money to see the museum, walk on the pier, and eat a huge, scrumptious seafood dinner. Maybe we'll do some shopping. You know she is going to Thailand in April. I wanted to be with her then, but of course she'll be out of town. That's my big news.

The future is going on with me and I am enjoying the still peace and relaxation and the blessings and gifts of Jesus. His mercy and grace—I count myself an extremely blessed girl to be enjoying the things that have always made me well—made me the happiest girl I can be. Don't worry about me, I'm going to go in a good frame of mind. The peace is overwhelming.

I really would like to see you, but I don't think I can. Keitha's baby is due in May. I go to bed as usual this time of evening so I'm going to read a little bit about the Holy Spirit and then just close my eyes and drift off to sleep. I love you, Jeanie. I will always love you. You are the closest and most dearest friend I have ever had in my whole life and I count myself truly blessed that I have a cousin who I trust. That means the world to me. Talk to you later. Miss you very much. Hugs and kisses. Hang in there, girl. Hope everything's going okay for you and I'm sure I'll hear from you soon . . . later . . .

CHAPTER 24

When His Breath Leaves Our Lungs

Miraculously my in-laws are in Florida visiting a relative only a couple of hours away at the same time I'm here.

Their trip had been planned months before, and the last time they had flown anywhere was two years before. This is so clearly providential. *I see You, God.*

They call me and ask me if I would like it if they came to be with me while I am with my mom. "Yes."

Once they arrive and after I fill them in, I ask my mother-in-law, Susan, if she will go with me to my mom's apartment. Gary, my father-in-law, will stay with my mom. I get my mom's keys from her purse and we drive to that beautiful building I had been in a year before.

Susan stands next to me as I slide the key into the doorknob and turn. We walk in, and I can smell her, an aroma of smoke and body spray and old books. She should be here, and we shouldn't be here without her. It's wrong. This is her space, her stuff, and what right do we have to just come in and go through it? But I'm leaving tomorrow and this might be my only chance to touch her things again, to feel her here. I also want to find her journals and photo albums, memories and thoughts that are recorded. Susan and I work our way through her things for about an hour and then we decide to go back to my mom.

Once we're back at the facility, a grief counselor visits us. She's small, pretty, put-together, elegant. She's probably in her fifties. She asks if we have any questions. I tell her no.

Susan has a question though. "I hear that gurgling in her lungs and it doesn't sound good. The doctor says she could take five to seven days to die, but that seems like a long time. What do you think?"

The woman furrows her brows and gently says, "Oh no, not with that sound. That's her lungs shutting down. She could go today."

Today? I could be with her? She won't have to die alone?

My in-laws hug me goodbye. They know I want it to be just my mom and me now.

I spread out pictures on the floor, pictures that show pieces of my mom's life. I lose track of time sitting on that floor, studying her life. The gurgling sound in her lungs stops. It's happening, she's leaving. I quickly gather the pictures and throw them in a box and pull a chair up to her bed. I hold her hand, rubbing my thumb over her rough, swollen skin. I put some music on, songs I know she loves, songs she had put on a CD for me years ago. "Sarah, you're the poet in my heart . . ."

"You give life, You give love, You bring light to the darkness. You give hope, You restore every heart that is broken. Great are You, Lord."

Over and over the same songs play quietly. Her eyes dart back and forth, and her breathing slows. Her eyes stop. I turn off the music and talk to her. I promise her I will tell our story, of what God has done. She always wanted to write, to help people, she said.

"You're almost there, Mom. Almost done. I'm right here with you. I love you."

My hand squeezes her hand and then I gently rub her head, her thin hair under my palms. And like a clock winding down, her breath just wound down. Slower and slower. I can feel her leaving.

And then, *her breath was gone.*

Just stillness.

On April 23, 2016 at 7:16 p.m. my mom took her last breath and entered the arms of Jesus.

She went from a father who wouldn't love her right into the arms of a Father who loved her unconditionally.

> "It's Your breath in our lungs, so we pour out our praise to You only, God."[5]

She Was Broken Too

If we all stepped out of our skin
out of our guts and bones
and saw into the soul
we'd see the histories and wounds and
fears and secrets
and we'd all know
we really aren't alone.

Mom's Journal | November 8, 1986 | Life as a single mom, trying so hard

I will list the reasons I tend to overlook that cause pain and anxiety:

1. The loss of Sarah

2. The lack of contact, day-to-day, with Sarah

3. A mother's pain of conceiving a child and living without her—that is intense itself

4. Responsibility for financial stability

5. Pressures of work aspects

6. Working with other women oblivious to my strain and pain

7. Conquering the hostile feelings from others, and from myself

8. Being healthy enough to maintain a stable working relationship

9. Responsibility of raising a two-year-old with PATIENCE and CONTROL. THIS IS RESPONSIBILITY AND CONTROL.

10. Living through this time with divorce and all the guilt feelings, inadequacy feelings, rejection, disappointment

11. Lack of communication with K

12. Verbal quiet attacks from K

13. Unawareness of final outcome due 11/18/86 (custody hearing)

14. Paranoia over secretiveness of proceedings

15. Lack of money for lawyer bills

16. Non-ability (desire) to keep house clean

17. Insecurity of "giving" and being needed by others

I think what's causing these overwhelming feelings of desperation are the factors involved in not knowing yet how all this divorce stuff will turn out. Now for the positive thoughts I must instill inside my poor, aching head . . .

1. Only one more week to November 18, after which I will know what the plan is for the future and K and Keitha

2. The release, as of then, of much uncertainty for my life

3. I will, as of then, let go of the memory of K and I and the possibility of going forward when the cancerous thoughts are holding me back

4. With "the end" so near, so close, I must grab hold and maintain, as there are only days to go.

5. Carol—a friend who loves me, cares about me, CAN IDENTIFY with me, and who is there for me, who I will visit today

6. Realize the importance of my position, which I handle well and regain PRIDE in myself for that ability.

7. Remember, it's going to be okay, because I'm going to make it okay by no longer letting all this get to me.

8. FIGHT against bad thoughts—overcome ill feelings—FACE THE CHALLENGE LIFE HAS GIVEN YOU—GROW IN THIS CHALLENGE—DON'T GIVE UP THE SHIP

9. With all this crap, the world can only get better—brighter—happier in the future.

10. Just think of how GOOD it's going to feel when the storm breaks—what may come with the new days and times could be marvelous!

11. Most of all, Susan, DON'T BE SO HARD on yourself. All this pain you're feeling is breaking your heart—of course! Be good to yourself. There's nothing wrong with the pain—you deserve it because it HURTS. Just keep it in perspective. IT HURTS, but it will also get better.

CHAPTER 25

Meeting My Mom

I don't sleep in my mom's apartment the night she dies.

I get a cheap motel room down the street. I crawl into bed and read the first journal I find, the one that's a yellow notepad that records the year 1986. On the cover is scribbled, "Read 10/10/08. SADNESS."

January 27, 1986. "32 years old, 3x's divorced, 2 kids, and 0 money."

I read the whole thing, and for the first time, I meet my mother.

––––––

After crying myself to sleep, I wake up, pack my things, and go to breakfast. I ask for a quiet, hidden spot, and begin reading more of her writing. *She was so complicated.*

I'm struck by how lonely she was. How desperately she wanted the love of her father. How broken she was after the molestation accusations and Keitha being taken and it was just *all too much.*

She was broken too.

Her father was a part of her breaking just as she was a part of mine. I longed for the love of a mother, and she longed for the love of a father.

Two broken girls, tangled up with each other, find their only hope not in the love of a mother or a father but in Jesus, who never left either of us. Jesus, who wooed us year after year until we surrendered. Mom may have taken longer to give that last bit of herself into His care, but she did it. If we're alive on this earth, it's not too late to bend a knee to the only One who can save us and love us completely and profoundly.

My heart is overwhelmed by regret. I wish I would have known the woman I met in her writings. Yes, I realize I have rose-colored glasses on right now, I admit that, but I still I wish I would have paid more attention. All I want to do now is hug her and visit her on holidays and send more pictures and Skype her with her grandkids. But I didn't do those things. I took the last years for granted.

Since I am utterly helpless to go back, to talk to her again, to love her more, I drive and scream. I'm driving this ridiculously small rental car up and down the highway screaming at the top of my lungs. The road is a blur. *Oh God, why didn't I know? And now it's too late.* I can't comfort her, or show her love, or make up for all the lost years.

Gene Knudsen Hoffman, a peace activist and Quaker, once wrote the famous phrase: "An enemy is one whose story we have not heard."[6] My mom was my enemy for years. She *was* cruel. What she destroyed in me was real, what she broke left scars. What she took, I can never have back. But, I am here, and my broken heart has been healed. The fire is long gone, and by God's grace and kindness and unwavering pursuit of my heart, the ashes that were left have turned to a garland of beauty and joy and hope and redemption. I am not the scared and helpless little girl I once was.

What I know now is that my mom was that little girl too. And I grieve for that little girl whose father's love was out of reach, whose heart was broken, and whose wounds were deep. I have compassion for the little girl inside the woman who found her relief in a bottle of vodka when the pain seemed unbearable.

I didn't turn to alcohol, but I had my demons. And I don't know why I was able to give my pain and addictions to God earlier in life while she was not. But I know that He never left her. And I know that had she been able to surrender all the pain to God in earlier years, He would have healed the places she was desperately afraid to face. Life could have been different, for her, for me, for my sister.

We all get the same choice in life: to stay in the pain, stiff-armed toward God, or to surrender all to Him. He pursues every one of us, and all we have to do is turn to Him and say, *Help. I surrender.*

Jesus died on a cross to cover every abusive word my mom spoke, every affection withheld, every foolish situation she put me in. All she had to do was accept it and turn her life over to Him. And she did.

There was victory in the end.

> People who are meaner than snakes have snake-bitten hearts. They have forgotten or perhaps never known they are loved beyond comprehension.[7] —Beth Moore

> Often I have been asked, "Brennan, how is it possible that you became an alcoholic after you got saved?" It is possible because I got battered and bruised by loneliness and failure, because I got discouraged, uncertain, guilt-ridden, and took my eyes off Jesus. Because the Christ-encounter did not transfigure me into an angel.
> —Brennan Manning,
> *The Ragamuffin Gospel*[8]

Mom's Journal | Date Unknown | Written after the death of *her* mom

My life has changed dramatically and now I realize that these changes would not have occurred if she were still here.

I didn't know. I didn't know how much her influence must have been to keep me in the direct family, since I'm no longer there. I deal with the guilt of my ignorance these days, how I could have been close to her if I'd only known she loved me. If she'd told me; if I'd seen it. Living with what my father has put me through since her death, things that hadn't happened when she was alive—duh— it was Mom who kept me safe, and all the while I thought it was him. These are just some of the thoughts I've been looking at, there's plenty more. "If there could just be some way to suck out all of these thoughts from my brain." At first, I was so angry, yet there was nothing I could do to stop it. I'd gone to bed at night, woken up in the middle of the night or very early morning with anger seething throughout my whole body, or remorse for my not knowing, or guilt for not seeing the invisible. Other nights, my breathing was labored, my heart palpitating, wheezing sound coming from my throat which had never happened before. I always took "pride" and satisfaction in how easy it was for me to rest peacefully. I began to believe that I was physically ill for real, a thought I'd never before entertained. Then I read "We are often ignorant of our needs, motivations, and conflicts" and "We must be sensitive to change in our health, sleep patterns, and dreams." I did not know, until reading these passages in the book that these sorts of disturbances happen with unwanted thoughts, I then realized that I was not "ill" in a bad physically way, I was having physical reactions to my mother's death and the conflicts resulting.

CHAPTER 26

Mourning the Loss of a Mother, Again

My kids know their grandma Suzy has died.

Jesse tells them gently, and he is kind. They didn't know her well; they were so little when she lived with us. But *I* feel it, and I don't want to hide my grief. I don't want to cry quietly into my pillow, making sure no one hears my sadness. I don't want to pretend that when someone close to you dies, you should just be fine. I want my kids to learn how to grieve so they don't feel like they have to hide.

Pain is not shameful, and neither is the vulnerability that comes with it.

I want to know how the people of God have grieved, if there is a process or a ritual or something. I'm not sure what exactly I'm looking for as I Google, "How did people in Bible times grieve?" I guess I don't want to feel alone. Maybe I just want to know how to grieve when I get home to my kids and neighbors and responsibilities and life.

I find a Jewish website on grieving. I learn that after a loved one dies, especially a parent, there are dedicated periods of mourning. These are meant to allow the mourner the full expression of grief and after various phases of intensity, eventually return to normal life.

The mourning period begins with the first seven days after a burial. During this seven-day period mourners stay home and don't go anywhere. This is so they can feel free to lament, unburdened by having to hide tears or explain themselves, or worse, pretend to be fine. When the tears come, there is no hiding, just a safe place to let it all out. The second time period which overlaps with the first is the thirty-day period. Mourners go back to work but refrain from going to parties or celebrations. The last time period is the twelve months after burial. This is done for a parent, and mourners avoid parties, celebrations, movies, and concerts. After the year, formal mourning is considered over.

Obviously, this is a *very* basic overview, but my goal isn't to follow the tradition perfectly, it's simply to gain some wisdom to help me through. And it does help. I have decided that when I get home, I'm going to cancel all obligations that I am able to cancel with integrity. I'm going to stay home and let the expression of grief have the freedom it desires.

Grieving in Front of My Children

My children hate seeing me sad or mad; they want me to be happy, to smile. They need to know that I'm okay because if I'm okay, their world is okay.

But what about the times it isn't okay? What happens when the walls cave in and the heart explodes and ache can't be hidden? What then?

How do I grieve in front of them without putting it on them?

Sometimes we carry our own childhood fears and experiences into our parenting without realizing it, and other times we are quite aware of it and we make vows to protect ourselves and our children. ("I will never let my kids see my sad or crying.") We believe we're protecting them, but I think maybe it's possible we're avoiding the opportunity to teach them about pain and grief and how to express it all. Sometimes we need to teach our kids how to be human, how to feel and process and not hide. How to be naked and unashamed in our grief.

There's wisdom in being aware and not laying our heavy burdens on little hearts not ready, but I think it's good and helpful and kind to let our children see our humanity and our grief and healthy ways of dealing with it.

I decide to let my children in on my grief.

I sit my children down and explain to them that I'm sad about Grandma Suzy, and that at times they are going to see me cry, but that I'm okay and it's normal and they don't have to worry about me or be afraid.

I tell them that showing sadness is nothing to be ashamed of.

I then hug each of my kiddos and tell them how very much I love them.

And then, when the grief hit randomly, and I cried, I didn't hide from them. I told them I would be okay; I wanted them to see the truth of grief so that one day, when they grieved, they would know it's not shameful or ugly or something to hide or run from. It's a part of life, of the human experience, of sin and death in this world—and also of the hope that one day there will be no more grieving or death, no tears or broken hearts. I want them to feel when they need to feel, cry when they need to cry, and scream into their pillow when the pain is too great and they feel like their whole body is going to explode from the fire of it all.

They can't learn how to do that if I hide it from them.

A Surprising Comfort

One thing I didn't anticipate in my grieving was the blessing of comfort my children would give me.

My youngest daughter, who was seven at the time of my mom's death, felt *with* me. One afternoon, during that first week of grieving, I was going through pictures of my mom and I started crying. My sweet little girl, who knew this was okay and normal and not going to last forever, held a little fabric angel in her hands that hospice had given me. She was looking at it, and at me, and she began to cry gently. She was feeling my ache. She came over, sat on my lap and hugged me, and we cried *together*. We both wept for the loss of Grandma Susy. Did my girl feel her own pain at the loss of her grandma? I'm sure, but she didn't know my mom, not really, because my mom moved away when my daughter was a toddler. But she felt and grieved anyway, and it was dear, *so* dear.

And after we cried and hugged, we wiped our eyes, kissed, and carried on; we were okay, together.

The gift of a child's comfort, I am convinced, is straight from the heart of God, their little arms showing us His arms. The comfort of a child is overwhelming and healing.

This is the gift of grief: the healing comfort experienced through the tender intimacy of shared vulnerability. And to experience this gift with your child is nothing short of a precious and rare grace.

An Acknowledgment of the Weirdness of Grief

It's the one-year anniversary month of my mom's death, and a strong gust of grief swirls over me. For whatever reason, this grief prompts me to get in my van and drive to the nearest grocery store. While tears are visibly streaming down my face, I look around and think, *I need a plant*.

I don't know why I feel the urge to buy a plant, especially since I am known for killing all plant life, but grief is weird and impractical, so I roll with it. I pick up a pretty, large-leafed plant (I have no idea what kind it is . . . still don't) and check out.

I get home and set my plant near a window and ponder it. I declare its name to be Suzy Hope. I'm completely aware of how weird this is, but like I said, grief is weird.

The plant is still alive over two years later. The name has shortened to just "Suzy." Every time we say something like, "Who watered Suzy?" we laugh.

And we all know, we can never let Suzy die.

Mom | Date Unknown | Found typed on a loose paper

I love you, dear Sarah, beyond what you may
  think.
Perhaps if long ago I'd gotten out the needle
  and thread,
the tools I'd need to sew my mouth shut,
what happened between us might never
  have been.

CHAPTER 27

Releasing My Vow

As a young woman, I vowed that I would never be like my mother.

But now that I'm older, I see that I can't escape my genes nor my history. I am a part of those who have gone before me. "Our lives are so important to us that we tend to think the story of them begins with our birth. First there was nothing, then *I* was born. . . . Yet that is not so. Human lives are not pieces of string that can be separated from a knot of others and laid out straight. Families are webs. Impossible to touch one part of it without setting the rest vibrating. Impossible to understand one part without having a sense of the whole."[9] Diane Setterfield wrote those words in her chilling book, *The Thirteenth Tale.*

This is true of course. So it is with my story and my mother and the knots that bind us together.

I *am* like my mother.

I carry in me the good *and* the bad (for lack of a better word). My mother was a writer. She loved art. She loved vocabulary. She had a quick mind, and she was sensitive and bold and sarcastic and hopeful. *She had great faith.* I see these attributes in myself. My mom also struggled with depression and feelings of failure and addiction. *Me too,* in my own ways. I wish I didn't, but it's a part of my story and possibly the story of my children and their children.

So I release my vow. *I couldn't keep it anyway.* Instead, I surrender myself to God, entrusting the good and the bad into His loving hands, the very hands that stretched out on a cross so I could come out of the dark and live in the light where there is victory.

CHAPTER 28

Dear Mom

Dear Mom,

I want you to know that *I know* you didn't know how to love me.

And yeah, you broke my heart, but you were broken too. I know. But that sweet redemption came in all its miraculous glory. *Thanking God for that.*

I put your ashes in the ground that July weekend and covered them in lavender under the forked tree with the cross carved into it.

Your ashes, your body, your bones, buried on a mountain. But not you. You are with Him because you never let go.

He saw right into your heart and He loved you, and you loved Him and it was such a weird thing, how you loved.

You were so *complicated*.

So layered.

So like a two-year-old, stubborn. But, oh, how you would laugh, loud and unedited. You sure could let it rip.

I had to grieve you twice, you know. The first time was when I had to acknowledge that I would never have a mom, not really. Not the kind of mom that nurtured. I released you from my expectation. I forgave you and do still. The second time was when your breath left your body, and the grieving is still present. I miss you, you know.

I just wanted a mom to love me, just like you wanted a father to love you, but you couldn't. I mean, you did; I know you did. But you didn't know how to show me. You were so broken, and I'm so sorry for all the pain you held up under. I would have broken too.

And I did, but not so bad. I was okay.

Your world was undone horrifically. And your mother-heart was bursting, I know, in a million pieces until it was just too much and you gave in to the thing that numbed you, that made you okay. I understand. I don't blame you now.

I read your journals.

I know how lonely you were.

How unloved you felt.

How defeated you were.

How you just wanted to not be a burden to anyone. So you hid your pain and your loneliness. God, I wish I would have known.

I wish I could have *really* known. I wish I saw you the way He saw you.

I'm so sorry.

But now, Mom, because of *you*, I want to love everyone because we are all so broken and so hidden, aren't we? Covered under pain that no one else sees.

We are all complicated in places and wounded, and we hurt because we hurt, and we love when we are loved, and *I will love*.

Because I know His love and how encompassing it is.

And you did, eventually.

You showed me at the end. He did that, I know.

Goodbye my beautiful, complicated, stubborn, free, mom. I know you are shining now.

And you are healed.

And you are basking in the love you always wanted and needed. How good our Father is.

I wish I could call you up. But I'll see you again one day.

I love you.

Addendum

From Darkness to Light | Susan Potts | August 2009

> The people who walked in darkness
> have seen a great light;
> those who dwelt in a land of deep
> darkness,
> on them has light shone.
> (Isaiah 9:2)

The verse above exemplifies the beginning of an incredible new journey that began when the doctor announced I had only two days of life left within me. According to him, the cirrhosis of my liver had progressed to the point of no return, and there was nothing that could be done. Thus, I began on my path in the shadow of death, leading me daily away from the darkness and toward the light; the most unexpected, spirit-filled, eye-opening, gracious, joyous journey I have ever had the pleasure to experience. So powerful is my journey that it is impossible for the mind to wrap around, no words to express the many endowments.

Jesus is with me every step of the way, and the truths He uncovers for me each day are overwhelmingly awesome. It is no less than a miracle that is happening within me due to His teachings. I am surely and truly blessed by God's grace.

I had unknowingly taken the first step of my mysterious journey a few weeks earlier when I heard "the voice" in my living room as I posed to take the first drink of the day, the usual, vodka and

7Up. "The voice" commanded me to put that drink down: *You do not need it, do not want it, do not even like the taste of it.* This was so powerful and true that I knew it was God, and I listened. Without taking a sip I rose from the couch, the untouched drink in my hand, headed to the kitchen sink, and poured it down the drain. Yes, I listened.

My hard drinking began somewhere in the mid-1980s, and barely a day went by without the ritual of preparing a drink and then drinking one after another until I was done for the evening. It had become routine, and I did not question the reasons.

I can proudly say that I have not had a drink since that "day of the voice." It has been over a year now and I no longer covet a drink. I have walked away from the darkness and into the light. That happened two weeks before my encounter with the hospital. Praise the Lord. I believe with all my heart that if I had taken that first gulp of liquor, mid-July 2008, I would have dropped dead then and there and left a shameful legacy for my two precious daughters, Sarah Mae and Keitha Marie. Praise Jesus, He saved them from that.

Well, that is the beginning of my story, a story my first-born child, Sarah, insisted must be written. There is plenty more—my life before being saved and after being saved is chock-full of a plethora of all kinds of stuff!

Thanks for listening, God bless you and keep you,

Susan Lynn Sherman Van Deilen Clark Messer Potts, the mother of a most precious and special daughter, Sarah Mae.

What Do I Do Now?

Pray this or something like it:

"God, here I am, bloody and bruised and weak. Please give me rest. Please speak to the intimate places of my soul and show me where I'm afraid to trust You, where I'm self-protecting, where I'm immovable. I will be thankful when I'm weak, because it means that You are so close to me and are resting on me and are filling me with all the power I need to do the hard things, the impossible things, like forgive when it feels unfair. You have forgiven me and loved me through all my leaving, all my doubt, and all the ways I've hurt You. Please show me when to walk away and when to stay, when to forgive, and when to wait. Thank You that You are always with me, always working good for me, and always about redemption."

Talk to a Safe Friend

Talk to someone about what God has revealed to you as you've read this book. What does He want you to see, believe, or do? Process all of this with your spouse, a counselor, or a trusted friend.

Go Deeper

If you want to go deeper into the themes that are in this book, I encourage you to go through the Bible study *Psalm 40: Crying Out to the God Who Delights to Rescue Us*, as seen in the back of this book.

For When You Think
It's All Impossible

For you, I offer this: Try changing, "I
    can't . . ." to, "With God, I can . . ."
I can't deal with this.
I can't face that.
I can't keep trying.
I can't do it.
I can't "go there."
I can't seem to get free from this thing.
I can't stop.
I can't stand them/her/him.
I can't forgive them/her/him.

With God, I can deal with this.
With God, I can face that.
With God, I can keep trying.
With God, I can do it.
With God, I can "go there."
With God, I can get free.
With God, I can stop.

With God, I can love them/her/him.

With God, I can forgive them/her/him.

With God, I can do all things through Christ who strengthens me.

Six Ways to Forgive (When You Don't Know What to Do with the Unfairness of It All)

1. Pray. Say to God, "Lord, I feel like this situation is so unfair and I feel so wronged and I don't know what to do with it, but I trust that You do know what to do with it. You know me, You know them, and You see all the things I don't. Plus, I know You love me and have my back (as well as theirs), so here You go, God, it's all Yours." In other words, trust God with the person and the situation.

2. Remember. Would you agree that life is hard? It is, and the fact is, nobody gets a free pass to skip the battle, not even the person who wronged you. When I remember that truth, that everyone is facing a hard battle, I can have compassion on the person who wronged me. Think also about all the times you have wronged someone. Yeah, that helps me to be more compassionate as well.

3. Ask. *Is there something I have done that I should ask forgiveness for with the person who wronged me?* Ask it. And ask without expectation that you will be asked for forgiveness in return. Free and clear, ask genuinely (ask God to show you where you may have gone wrong/offended).

4. Choose. Choose to be a person of the light. The enemy wants nothing more than to keep you in the dark—seething, feeling vengeful, getting worked up, having major lack of peace—he wants you far away from forgiveness, because forgiveness shines blindingly, beautifully bright.

5. Seek. Seek outside help from wise and kind mentors and/or counselors. God in His kind provision gave people gifts of counseling, and we can reap such healthy rewards through the help of others. I would not be where I am today if it weren't through the gentle help of so many others. Don't try and heal on your own.

6. Evaluate. Evaluate the relationship you're in. Is it twisty and consuming, manipulative, unhealthy, and/or just messed up? Take some time to honestly assess the situation and the relationship. You can forgive and still set boundaries or make a clean break if necessary. Pulling away for a time can be especially helpful and wise so you can get yourself in a healthy place, so you can forgive and love well, whether that is up-close or from a distance.

How to Work through Your Core Lies[10]

By Dave Bowman

1. Remember events. Look back to the events in your life where you can pinpoint hurts and pains. These events often involve people who were or are important (parents, friends, coaches, teachers, relatives, siblings, authorities, etc.). Write out or verbalize as much as you can remember about these moments or events . . . the words, thoughts, emotions, and so on.

2. Recognize that you have been sinned against (you might not be totally aware of it). Acknowledge that another (or others) have wronged you through their own sin and lack of love toward you and it did hurt. Come to a point where you are willing to admit your disappointment in relationships with your mother, father, brother, sister, coach, etc. (Rom. 8:18–24).

3. Response. How did you respond to the event(s) and/or to the relationship(s)? With anger? Withdrawing? Helpless feelings? Embarrassed? Feeling abandoned? Feeling controlled? Recognizing your past responses may help you see why you now relate to and respond to people the way that you do.

4. Realize your emotional response. Look at your present-day painful events and how you respond to them. What are your emotions? What recent situations, conversations, or thoughts cause you to feel angry, anxious, or depressed? Keep a journal, record whatever promotes such feelings, and consider these questions as you consider the event(s): What was said in the situation? What did you see? What were you concerned/afraid would happen? Were you concerned or afraid that something would not happen? Did you feel threatened at all? If so, what felt threatening? What part of you felt threatened (your intelligence, your character, your appearance, etc.)? When you were feeling angry, anxious, or depressed, what judgment or conclusion of you were you concerned people would make? Was there a concern in you that people would view you in a certain way if this didn't go well? What were you concerned they would see you as?

5. Reveal your goals (allow God to do this; look at your emotions). Consider what the red lights on your dashboard reveal and what prompted these feelings (your analysis above on #4). You have a goal that you are trying to reach. What is your goal? Are you demanding that others view you in a certain way (as competent, good, etc.)? Are you demanding that others treat you in a certain way? Are you pressuring yourself to present yourself to the world in that same way (you want to be seen in this way in order to avoid pain)? In order to achieve this goal, you have imposed an unbreakable law on yourself ("I must do . . ." and "I must be . . .") and on others ("You must view me as . . ." and "You must treat me as . . ."). This is not God's law, but your own, selfish law. What do you do? Recognize that you have chosen your response to the sin and the hurts you've experienced from others. Recognize and "own" (admit to yourself and God) your manipulative and self-protective behaviors. Identify and recognize that you have set up these goals for a purpose.

6. Relating a certain way behaviorally. Look for self-protection or manipulation strategies and behavior in your relationships. Ask yourself, "Why do I behave toward people a certain way?" Ask others what "pulls" do they feel from you? How do they feel they need to come through for you? If you feel pressure to behave a certain way, this is the time to ask, "Why am I doing what I'm doing?" We must see our sinful strategies of manipulation and self-protection as sin. We must repent of these. Examples of self-protection ("abandon") strategies: abandonment/ quitting, avoidance, going to something else (TV, porn, eating, etc.), acting shy or silly, etc. Examples of manipulation ("abuse") strategies: flattery/charm, anger/bully, moodiness, performance/competitive, being sarcastic or argumentative, etc. These relating styles are chosen to avoid the hurt, pain and subsequent feelings—anger, surprise, helplessness, and so on—that you have experienced in the past. Some examples of styles of relating: bully, silly, charmer, shy, avoider, loner, quiet, sarcastic, intellect, one-upmanship, debater, competitor, etc.

7. Renounce vows, lies, and images. Are there vows that you have made when you were hurt (e.g., "I will never be embarrassed like that again.")? These vows need to be brought before God and renounced. You need to discover the lies that you believe about yourself and the vows you made. These lies are deep within you, which is why we call them "core lies." You may begin to discover your personal core lie by considering what your main goal is. Also, going back to initial painful events, ask God to tell you what lie you believed in that painful event. We need to have a changed mind (Rom. 12:1-2). We need to form ideas of who we are based on what God says in His Word. What do we do? Identify and articulate your core lies (a core lie forms a goal which affects behavior). Realize that these core lies control you. These lies dictate your relating style (your thoughts, words, and actions) with everyone (to varying degrees) including God. Discover your image—how you truly view yourself. This is difficult to recognize at times, but it is often a type of person (wimp, loser) or a certain animal or image (worker ant, baby bird, etc.). To help identify your image, look at the context in which your core lies were formed. Look at your vows—what you said you would never or always do. Again, renounce these things as lies about who you are.

8. Repent of your goal (false self/idol/demanding spirit). Acknowledge who you are in Christ and that only He will fulfill your deepest longings. Realize that the emotions, beliefs, behavior, goals, and images are your slave masters. They have put you in bondage. The focus of these areas is *self*, and the Bible calls this pride. One must choose to repent of these idols (goals) and choose to turn from them. This repentance is seen when one realizes he or she has a choice to depend on self (protect themselves or manipulate others) or to depend on God. When depending on God you are able to move toward another in love without the demands for them to come through for you in order to make your false identity secure. Ask God to forgive you for the pride that is in you as you have been driven to pursue your false self or goal more than your desire to know Him.

9. Replace. The lies must be replaced with God's truth. For each lie, ask God what the truth is and then, in prayer, nail the lie on the cross of Jesus or give the lie to God and ask Him to replace it with His truth, which is found in the Bible. If you need help finding the truth or understanding it, ask someone who knows the Bible. Reach out to wise mentors and kind and safe Christians, and they will help you.

10. Reconcile/Restore. There are relationships that have hurt you. You might need to thank God that He died for the sin they committed against you so that you don't have to carry that weight around with you or the emotional pull that it can have on you. Forgive those who have hurt you. Reconcile with those whom it is wise or possible to reconcile.

Acknowledgments

Keitha—You are brave and beautiful and I'm so grateful you're my sister.

Don Jacobson—Thank you for making a dream come true for me.

Jennifer Lyell—Thank you for wanting this book and for giving me the time to write it so it could be what it was meant to be.

Ashley Gorman—Thank you for being such an encouraging editor and a delight to work with.

Mary Wiley—Thank you for giving me lists and keeping me on task. You are fantastic at your job.

Jade Novak—Thank you for the beautiful and fitting cover you designed. I think my mom would have loved this cover.

Adriana Badoi—Thank you for your beautiful artwork of the thistle on the cover of the book. You are so gifted.

Dave and Cathy Bowman—Thank you for teaching me about core lies and for being a part of changing my life.

Melanie Harding—Thank you for helping me to grieve the loss of a mother. Learning to let her go set me free.

Katelyn Bailey—Thank you for being such a faithful caregiver to my kids in the summer so I could work on this book. You are so dear to our family.

Kimberley Knockel—Thank you for teaching me to get curious instead of judge myself. I cannot tell you how often this reorients my thoughts to one of healing and hope instead of despair.

Janet Mylin—Thank you for helping me get clarity with this book and my message.

Amy, Logan, Robyn, Jen, and Lynn—Thank you for being faithful, supportive friends, always encouraging me and spurring me on toward truth and grace and goodness.

Dad—Thank you is too small of a thing to say in comparison to how big your love was in my life and how it saved me in so many ways. You will forever hang the moon in my world.

Gary and Susan—Thank you for your support and encouragement. Your steadfast love for me is felt and is a gift from God.

Jesse—Thank you for being my biggest supporter, my pep talk coach, and my safe place.

Ella, Caedmon, and Caroline—Thank you for being gracious and kind and so loving to your imperfect mother. You all are my favorites.

About the Author

Sarah Mae is the author of several books, including *Desperate: Hope for the Mom Who Needs to Breathe* (with Sally Clarkson). She resides in Lancaster County, Pennsylvania, with her husband and three children.

You can find her online at http://sarahmae.com.

Follow The Complicated Heart conversation:

Instagram.com/TheComplicatedHeart

#TheComplicatedHeart

The Complicated Heart podcast at sarahmae.com/thecomplicatedheart podcast

Notes

1. Let the reader note that the use of the phrase *retarded* was included in efforts to quote this conversation accurately, but in no way communicates my approval of the phrase. I would never use it in normal conversation, nor do I think anyone else should, as I believe in dignifying the image of God in every person.

2. "I Found Myself in You," from the album Time to Believe by Clay Crosse, 1995.

3. Henry Cloud and John Townsend, *Boundaries: When to Say Yes, How to Say No to Take Control of Your Life, Updated and Expanded* (Grand Rapids, MI: Zondervan, 2017).

4. Ibid.

5. "Great Are You, Lord," David Leonard / Jason Ingram / Leslie Jordan.

6. Citation can be linked to an essay by Gene Knudsen Hoffman, the *Journal of The Fellowship of Reconciliation*, May/June 1997, https://www.compassionatelistening.org/product-page/compassionate-listening-and-other-writings -essays-by-gene-knudsen-hoffman.

7. https://twitter.com/BethMooreLPM/status/879695327 711907840

8. Brennan Manning, *The Ragamuffin Gospel* (Sisters, OR: Multnomah, 2005).

9. Diane Setterfield, *The Thirteenth Tale* (New York: Simon & Schuster, 2006), 58.

10. Dave Bowman's advice in this book is from a presentation he gave on Core Lies.